NEVER TR[GROWN MAN WITH A PONYTAIL

HOW A REGULAR GUY LIVED A ROCKSTAR LIFE

By

Jay Nachlis

TABLE OF CONTENTS

PREFACE

This life and the book's recollection of such would not have been made possible without the unwavering support of my wife, Jennifer. Every time she started a career path, we moved to another city for my nutty radio dreams and derailed hers. My love and appreciation for her cannot be measured.

To my mom, who bought the Panasonic recorder and Radio Shack cassettes. To the person at Enterprise for High School Students who assigned me the internship at X100. To everyone at X100 who could have made it an uneventful internship but instead gave a teenager the chance of a lifetime. To the greatest college radio station and classroom on Earth, Z89. To Syracuse University. Orange forever. To NewCity Communications, the company that invited a kid in his early 20's to attend big corporate strategy sessions. To Steve Marcus. To Alan Furst, my first mentor and king of the sushi lunch. To Casey Keating, for giving me a shot in San Francisco. To Ryan Seacrest, you have no idea how much your work ethic inspired me. To Jeff Silver, for the most valuable management lessons. To Buffalo, and to Doug Dombrowski for welcoming me like no other. To Peter Connolly for the Motor City shot. To Detroit – home of the greatest, most fiercely loyal, kindest, and toughest people I have ever known. To Phil Zachary and Mike Hartel for hiring me in Raleigh. To Raleigh. After hopping town to town, up and down the dial, you became my grown up home. To Kenny Kaplan and Paul O'Neill of Trans-Siberian Orchestra. Your generosity knows no bounds. Whenever I asked you to support a charitable cause that was important to me, you did. To Lou Rizzo, Nick Bedding, Jocelyn Taub, Jo Hodge, and all the amazing record reps with whom I shared these experiences along the way. To

Scott Aaron, for allowing me to grow and expand the limits. To Dave Rose, President of Deep South Entertainment and unofficial mayor of Raleigh. You have been an incredible promotional partner, career inspiration, and great friend. I owe you an debt of gratitude for helping me get to get over the hump and release this book.

Finally, to everyone who believed (and still believes) in me and all those I call friends. This dream isn't possible without you, and I'm fortunate to have you in my life.

DON'T SKIP THE INTRODUCTION

Every person who has worked in the music industry says that they are going to write a book someday. "The stories I could tell!" The truth is, we *all* have great stories – it's just that not all of us write them down.

It occurred to me as I wrote this book that it almost all takes place before I turned 30, mostly between 1988 and 2002. The first reason is that I had my first of two kids when I was 31. The vast majority of the things I experienced before 30 would have never happened if I was a father. The second reason is that the industry has changed. I got into radio when record companies regularly flew program directors to conventions. There was the leading trade newspaper, Radio and Records, but there was also "Hits" and "Network 40" (on which even lil' ol me graced the cover) and a slew of other rags that have gone by the waste side. The radio industry I joined saw itself on par with Hollywood. We were part of the entertainment mecca. We had Howard. We were inventive and dynamic. Competition between local radio stations in similar formats (before mega companies bought and brought the competitors under one roof) could be fierce- from slashed tires on a station van to showing up at the other team's events. Most of all, it was fun. Really, really fun.

When I look back now, radio was destiny for me but it was for many of us. Talk to a radio DJ and ask them if they ever called request lines when they were kids just to talk to their favorite personality. Ask them if they ever recorded themselves pretending to be on the radio (I used the old Radio Shack Tandy cassettes in the Panasonic recorder with the orange record button). Ask them if they talked up the post (the musical intro to a song before the vocal begins) in the family station wagon on weekend trips when a song came on the radio. (That, incidentally, is why my Twitter handle is @talkupthepost). Ask them if, when they first started in radio, they ever had the "dead air dream". The one where the music stops and the control board is there within your sight to press the button to fire the next song, but is just out of your reach.

This book is a celebration and a thank you letter. It is a joyful trip to the very strange world of radio - and a genuine debt of gratitude for the greatest job in the world.

CHAPTER 1

THIS BOOK ALMOST NEVER HAPPENED

Our story begins on the day of J Eugene McAteer High School's Senior Prom, 1990. It was overcast in the Diamond Heights district of San Francisco, which sits under the looming presence of Sutro Tower, the City's gargantuan 977 foot three-pronged red and white antenna that transmits a huge chunk of the Bay Area's television and radio stations. When you drive down the hill from the tower, you may end up on Portola Drive. Take a left, and follow it through downtown as it turns into Market Street and end up at the Ferry Building on the Bay. Take a right, and follow it until it turns into Sloat Blvd. through the Sunset district and end up at the San Francisco Zoo, adjacent to Ocean Beach. Look straight ahead and you'll see a tremendous valley in which now lies the Ruth Asawa School of the Arts. On the day of the Senior Prom, that was J Eugene McAteer High School, and the street next to that was where it happened.

O'Shaughnessy Boulevard is a road that winds along the side of this valley in which my high school called home, and connects Portola Drive with the Glen Park district, in which I called home. On this day, I had just picked up a corsage from a florist in the Sunset to pin on the dress of a girl I had not yet met. I was an extremely shy kid. So shy with the ladies, in fact, my mother once asked me if I was gay (not that there's anything wrong with that). So shy, that a friend hooked me up with a blind date for my Senior Prom. There I was, cheek to cheek grin, cruising along in my 1968 VW Beetle that I learned how to drive in on the hills of San Francisco (so trust me when I tell you that I can drive a stick shift *anywhere*). I crossed Portola Drive and descended upon the curvy jolts of

O'Shaugnessy. As a 17-year old may be apt to do, I sometimes drove a little too fast. Generally speaking, "a little fast" was manageable if the weather conditions allowed. By this point, however, the overcast skies had included high winds and sideways rain in its repertoire and 45 miles an hour down this hill was not a great idea.

I don't remember what the outside looked like when I started spinning, just that everything was spinning so rapidly. *Turn into the slide? Turn away?*   I thought that for a moment, but it didn't matter. The Bug spun so fast, so quickly there was no controlling it. All I could do was put my arms on the wheel and my head in my arms to try to stop the nausea and wait. Thud.

I looked up. I wasn't dead. I hadn't crashed into another car. At least I was pretty sure, I didn't see one next to me. When I looked to my left, I saw the valley below. To the right was the street, with cars driving up and down. One would stop and offer to drive to a pay phone to call my mother and tell her to come. In the meantime, I emerged from the car and realized that aside from a sprained finger and some back and neck pain, I apparently had incurred no major injuries. The car was essentially totaled, but remarkably the little buggy that could with its old school seat belts that didn't lock protected me from harm. Incredibly, as I had spun around and across O'Shaugnessy – *across the lane of traffic that comes up the hill* – I'd managed to avoid a collision with another vehicle. What was most remarkable of all was what I discovered next – where my car had perched in its final resting place. The car had managed to wedge itself in between two guardrails – the only small portion of the entire guardrail system on that street in which two guardrails overlap in that way. There were plenty of other areas of the hill in which I may have hit a guardrail and careened back into the street, where an oncoming car could have obliterated me. There are plenty of areas on the hill in which, frighteningly, there is no guardrail at all – at which I may have tumbled into the valley below to near certain death.

I don't know why I was spared that day. I can't be sure it was God, but then again I can't be sure that it wasn't. What I do know is that if my car hadn't found the wedge, this book, my wife, my kids, my life – may have never transpired. For that, I am eternally grateful.

CHAPTER 2

FM RADIO? WHAT'S THAT?

June, 2011. The moment happened in the Swami Cab ride on the way from the music industry conference in Carlsbad to visit a college friend at a house party just down the road in Cardiff-By-The-Sea, in the San Diego area of California. Iggy Pop was the culprit. Damn you, Iggy Pop and your Stooges. This business has treated me well for my entire adult life. In fact, it's treated me well since I was a teenager. It's paid the bills (sometimes). I've partied with rock stars, seen just about every concert I wanted to see for free, started a band, and now Iggy Pop, you have me questioning my future when this business is the only one I've really ever known. Truth is, you can't fight the future – and if the road forks, you better take it or make your own path. Of course, if Iggy Pop ever heard me spout a cliché like that he'd beat me to a bloody pulp.

Let's be honest. It wasn't even Iggy's fault, it was Mark the Swami Cab driver. When I hopped in the taxi, Iggy was playing. No, not "Lust For Life" for god's sake – "I Wanna Be Your Dog". When I glanced at the radio, 89.7 was the frequency glowing in a greenish-blue and I wasn't familiar with that station. "What station are you listening to?", I asked Mark the Swami, expecting him to school me about some hipster college station out of La Jolla that was spinning the freshest jams on Saturday nights. He would tell me about how he grew up in Southern California in the early 80's, when Circle Jerks and Dead Kennedys ruled the roost. Now on 89.7 on Saturday nights, it takes him back to high school to relive the grand days of SoCal punk. That is what I expected him to say. Here's what I did not expect him to say...

Pandora.

Pan-fucking-dora.

OK, look. I don't have any problem with Pandora. I enjoy it, though I'm partial to Amazon Music and Spotify. That year, when I listened to a Duran Duran channel on Pandora I was treated to commercials for a gay dating service. I can only gather Pandora assumed at the time that if you're a male listening to Duran Duran, there is no way in hell that you are straight. Not that there's anything wrong with that.

I don't even take issue with the fact that everyone was starting to buy smartphones (I had just been reminded of this at the industry conference) and that makes it really easy for everyone to get access to Pandora on their phone and that means that they can plug a cable into the auxiliary jack in their car. If they already had something like the new Ford Sync, they had that little "P" app right in front of them or can get it wirelessly through Bluetooth. Meanwhile, FM radio is banished to the side like some sort of relic in a music history museum.

I take issue with the fact that Mark the Swami is listening to Pandora instead of radio. The question had to be asked. "Why don't you listen to FM Radio?", I ask innocently. Before I even broached the question I knew what the answer was going to be, so asking the question was like asking to be placed into a freaking torture ride that I've already been on over and over and over again. Ok, brace yourself. Go ahead, Swami, say it. "Because FM Radio is lame".

Should I have been surprised? Not really, because FM Radio is, in fact, sometimes lame. Our tale starts with the radio ratings monopoly Arbitron (which has since been purchased by Nielsen, because why not a total monopoly on media ratings?). When you work in radio, you get asked all the time why playlists aren't more diverse. Why it is that we play the same 200 songs on repeat. Why, for crissake, "Stairway to Heaven" has to come out of the speakers twice daily like our lives depended on it. Why? Because you told us to!!! What? NO I DIDN'T! YES YOU DID! NO I DIDN'T! YES, YOU DID! Well, no you didn't. "You" didn't, you're right. Because "you" are not the listener. "You" are not who radio stations are programmed for. "You" would not, in your right mind, carry around a diary that looks like one of those blue books you used to take tests on in college for a week and fill out, in 15 minute increments, every station you listened to. For a dollar or two. Unless you're in a hard to reach demographic, like young males or African Americans, then you might get 5 dollars or more. No? You wouldn't do that? Why, because you have a LIFE?

Exactly.

But these people that fill out radio diaries often don't do it right and it is not their fault. Since nobody in their right mind would actually carry around a diary in their pocket or purse and write down the station they were listening to at that time, they fill it out how you and I would fill it out. At the end of the week, when it is time to return the diary....no that's too generous an assumption. You may get a grace period of a few weeks in which to return the diary. So let's say at the end of a couple weeks, after a week has gone by since the week you were supposed to track your radio listening, that's when most of these people that aren't in their right mind fill out their diary.

I don't even remember what I had for lunch **today**.

So, as we like to say in the business (and by the "business" I do mean the "business"), Nielsen measures based on a recall system instead of actual listening. So if the person filling out the diary remembers you, you're in luck. If not, sorry. SOL. I vividly remember a radio executive telling us in a staff meeting that if one of us were to get a diary, "you know...uh...I mean...you know. what I'm saying is...(shoulder shrug and pause for dramatic effect) is what I'm saying." Cue staff laughter. Radio people have been fired for filling out diaries. It's not illegal, but it is unethical. Ratings methodology has been a frustration for many a radio person over the years and Arbitron has been on the record acknowledging the response rate problem. In January, 2016, the Media Rating Council threatened Nielsen's diary-based ratings system with loss of accreditation if issues aren't corrected.

Good ol' Arbitron figured out a better way though, but only for the top 50 U.S. markets by population. It's called PPM, which stands for Personal People Meter. This little device actually measures radio listening by itself! Which is great, except for the fact that for example, according to an unofficial study conducted by radio host Allen Kepler and research firm Broadcast Architecture, some panelists have been documented cheating to make it appear that they are moving by attaching the device to a ceiling fan. That's part of the deal – you have to do a certain amount of moving throughout the day to make sure you're not just letting it sit at home or work capturing what's on the radio in the room. And then there's the fact that many of the panelists aren't participating because they care that their opinions matter – they may be only doing it for the money and fabulous rewards points (do you think this benefits stations that can afford to give away money?) There's the landline problem – it was easy (insert your own air quotes around easy) for Arbitron during the landline era – but more challenging with mobile phones and everyone having caller ID. And the dastardly do-not-call list! Much tougher, so sample sizes got lower and lower. And there's the fact that the device looks like a pager, because Arbitron started developing this technology when people still wore pagers. The biggest problem with the meter is the sample sizes. As a Program Director in Raleigh thanks to a program called Media Monitors, I could view the listening patterns of meter holders and watch how they utilized our station in real time. At any given time, it appeared you're lucky if 5-10 people are listening to your station at once.

Wait...what?

My career, my livelihood was based on the listening habits of 5-10 people?

Yes.

Let's go back to Mark the Swami who is listening to Iggy Pop on his Pandora channel. Mark thinks FM Radio is lame. Except that FM Radio in San Diego is not lame. It had multiple alternative stations that would play music, at least theoretically, he should enjoy. Since I got to town for this conference, I'd spent my time listening to one station in particular that played *early* Black Keys (they didn't break out until their newer "Brothers" album), a Jane's Addiction song I had never heard of but thoroughly dug, the Foo Fighters single that just came out that week, and, for crying out loud, "Time To Get Ill" from the Beastie Boys. When I mentioned this station to the Swami, he agreed they were good. He mentioned a Saturday night specialty show that they he loves from 10pm-1am. The host, he told me, was incredible. Which is all fine and good, except I was in his cab at that time and we were listening to....Pandora. If FM Radio can't get this guy to listen, who *are* we going to get to listen?

I held out some hope. I thought to myself that if there's a commercial FM station like this playing Jane's Addiction and Beastie Boys deep tracks, maybe their ratings were good. Maybe people's (by "people" I mean these few special folks that fill out diaries and carry meters), tastes are coming around and there's hope for a station like this! I took a look that day. Their ratings were not good.

CHAPTER 3

THE FIRST TASTE OF THE RADIO DRUG

It was 1988 and I was 15 ½ when I found out about an internship program for high school students in San Francisco that was one of the only ones of its kind. For as long as I could remember, I wanted to be a sports broadcaster. I looked up to Hank Greenwald, who did play-by-play for the San Francisco Giants, and idolized Chris Berman on ESPN. I loved his baseball nicknames so much (George "Taco" Bell...Gary "US Bonds" Puckett, etc.) that I would regularly make my own. Kevin "my SEITZER on the ball" was one of my favorites. Gary "Shopping" Carter was another. So when word came down that one of the internships available was at the one and only KNBR in San Francisco – the station that carried my beloved Giants – well, you can just imagine the murals I started painting in my head. I saw myself in the booth at Candlestick Park, during Giants games in the summer, researching stats for Hank. Sometimes, in between innings, he would teach me inflection and show me tricks for memorizing the names and numbers of players. When the internship was over, Greenwald would be so impressed with his young apprentice that he would personally call his Alma Mater, Syracuse University, and offer up his personal recommendation. After attending the prestigious S.I. Newhouse School of Public Communications, where Bob Costas and Marv Albert got their start, I would be hired full time by KNBR and I would be the youngest person ever to host their own sports talk show.

Except it didn't work out that way.

I certainly applied for the gig at KNBR, but I was offered

the internship at KXXX, a fledgling Top 40 station called X100. Boy, was I pissed. I think I was more sad and hurt than pissed. No, pissed first, then sad and hurt. I know I was pissed because I told my mom I wasn't going to accept. "I don't want to be a DJ!!!!", I told her. "I want to be a sports broadcaster!!" Side note: What kind of 15 year old is so sure about what he wants to do for the rest of his life? Like a good mom should do, she talked me off the proverbial ledge. She thoughtfully explained to me that regardless of what kind of station it was, this was an opportunity to try out the industry and see if it was something I would enjoy. It doesn't necessarily have to be something you do for the rest of your life, she told me, but give it a shot and you just might enjoy it. So, I gave it a shot.

If you want to make a good impression on a kid about your industry, have a team of DJs with long hair and cool clothes and music blaring out of speakers everywhere you turn. Have plaques of gold records everywhere. Have phones that light up and on-air lights that flash and have Will Smith (then known as The Fresh Prince) visiting the studio when he arrives.

The fact is, I was mesmerized by X100 from the first minute I set foot in the place. It was in a seven story building right in front of one of the pagoda-adorned entrances to San Francisco's legendary Chinatown. How do I remember it was seven floors? You never forget what floor you were on during a 7.1 earthquake (but that comes later). The entrance was bright and colorful, the logo of the station aggressive and bold with red, black, and yellow. There was a couch in front of the receptionist desk where I would later discover many a DJ would pass out on. The endless cubicle world of the sales department occupied the bottom floor, but up the stairs was...magic. There were studios with huge glass windows you could peek into. On the other side of the studios was an immense view of downtown San Francisco. There were people with long hair walking around, and their pictures were on the walls. Speakers everywhere blared the sounds of Huey Lewis and the News. There was a giant siren I could spot inside the main studio that blared and flashed every time the competition, KMEL, had dead air. (In those occasions, I would find out, the DJ was to play a piece of imaging that said..."When they're nappin', we're jammin'!" or when the other station was in talk and we were in music, "When the others are talkin'...we're rockin'!") The amount of responsibility they gave me was astounding. I was even paid! $1,500 for the summer. I haven't paid an intern once, and I've been a Program Director since the mid-90's! I started working in the research department. I would call people and ask them if they would be willing to listen to some song hooks and rate them by pressing a number on their phone. For some reason, the only song I remember testing was "Paradise City" by Guns N Roses (it tested well). I took on more responsibilities, including working as a producer for the Afternoon Drive show. This involved answering the request lines, screening the calls, and pulling carts for the next hour of music. In the late 80's, all the music and commercials were on "carts", which looked like 8-track tapes. I would look at the music log that had been generated by the Music Director, and would pull all the next hour's music so the DJ had it ready to put in the cart machines.

The first DJ I worked with was not fond of people being in his space. He very much liked to work alone. I was in his studio pulling carts when I reached over his shoulder and pulled one of the carts out of the on-air machine, thinking he was done with it and I would be helpful by putting it away. Only problem was, he wasn't done with it. He was about to play it in 10 seconds. He grabbed it forcefully out of my hand, put it back in the machine, gave me an evil eye, then calmly opened up the mic and did his break. As soon as the break was over, he spun around and let me have it. "WHERE THE FUCK DO YOU GET OFF?", I remember him saying. I don't remember the rest, but there was a whole lot more of that word, and an S-word, and an A-word, a D-word, and other subjugations of the English language that included curse words that may have not previously existed. Mind you, I had only been an intern for a short period of time. It was horrifying and I was sure I was going to get fired. Someone got fired, all right – but it wasn't me. So imagine the guilt of thinking I was some lowly intern that got this big-time radio guy fired. They told me it wasn't because of that, but I'm not so sure. I always wondered how the higher ups found out, because I didn't tell them. It's entirely possible, despite the impressive soundproofing, that the incident could have been and likely was heard down the hall and perhaps even across the bay in Oakland. Suffice it to say, I was told by someone in the programming department that it wasn't his first episode. Maybe they'd simply been looking for a way to get rid of the guy and that was all they needed. The last paper in the file.

CHAPTER 4

THE HAUNTED GOLD MINE SPECIAL TOUR

Much like how Times Square in New York City is now lined with chain stores like Toys R Us and Hershey's, San Francisco's Fisherman's Wharf didn't always show off with Rainforest Café and Build-A-Bear. In the day, the Wharf was dirtier, dingier, and full of tourist traps like the Haunted Gold Mine.

For around $7 per adult and $5 per kid, a family could enter and visit a fake underground gold mine. There were fake moving prospectors! An elevator ride that made you feel like you were in a mine shaft! If you were really lucky, you'd run into a couple of tour guides that would offer to take you on the "special tour" for the low, low price of five additional dollars (that covered the entire family! Such a deal!) The only problem was, although they were real people, they were not real tour guides. They were two teenage boys looking to bilk tourists while they were already in the moment.

Let's just say I was an entrepreneur.

First and foremost, my BFF Deion and I were very well versed in the teachings of the Haunted Gold Mine. We had been down there so many times that, regardless of the real history of the place (which we knew from reading the back of the brochure...that they give everyone when they buy their tickets), we had formulated extensive stories about these mines and the people within. We would talk about Ol' Harrison who, in 1849, lost a limb while prospecting for gold right on the spot you're standing, We'd tell tales of the elevator that fell 20 stories to its demise, taking 10 miners with it to a dusty grave. (We told that story while one of us was in the elevator and the other was outside shaking it. It was a pretty cool effect).

Over the course of a few weeks, we entertained about 20 families, and the payoff was always the same. We'd take our loot to the video arcade (it's a Hard Rock Café now) and play Ms. Pac Man, Donkey Kong, and Skee Ball til we couldn't see straight. Those really were the days – you got 8 tokens for a dollar, and each game took only one token. Amazing. Who knows how long our scheme would have lasted if it weren't for the family that asked the manager if the tour guides were legit.

Oh well. They were ripping people off, and we were just ripping them off a little more. Though, for entertainment value, I think our tour was better than the self-guided version.

CHAPTER 5

SPANK YOU VERY MUCH

As a parent in my forties with two young children, there are obviously moments of insanity. Yet my mother and my wife's parents like to say things like, "You were never that badly behaved." At first, I would get angry. Indignant. I was really that perfect of a child, huh? Plus, that kind of comment makes you feel like you are a terrible parent because you can't keep your kids in line. But as the years go by, I think the comment wasn't malicious. And I don't believe it was true. I think our parents either flat-out forgot what pissers we were or they selectively and subconsciously removed it from their memories.

Comparatively, I think I was a pretty good kid. But I forgot how often I was not. The ages of 16 and 17, when I was working at X100, profoundly affected the rest of my life and certainly my career path – but all the kids at my high school (many of which had no inkling of the rockstar life I was living) thought I was a dork with no social skills. I am a dork. Every radio person is a dork. As for social skills, it was true that I had a really hard time fitting in at my high school though I tried incessantly. Case in point: trying out for the basketball team during my junior year.

The McAteer Jaguars were stocked with talent that year. We had three players who were McDonalds All-American team candidates. We had plenty of guys who could dunk, pass, shoot with touch, play nasty defense – the whole package. I would never be a starter on this team, but I was decent enough that I thought I could earn a bench spot. On one of the first days of tryouts, another player stepped on my foot during sprints. I felt it burn and should have sat down right then and there. But, no guts no glory. So I kept practicing for the next two hours during what was primarily an endurance challenge with lots of running. When I got home that night, my foot was black and blue and it hurt like someone had pressed on it with a hot iron. To the hospital, to the X-ray machine, to the results....broken foot.

Though my basketball career seemingly ended before it began, the coach offered me the position of team "manager", which generally meant I got to carry equipment around. But, when my foot healed, I practiced with the players (some of which I regularly beat one-on-one). I was the first one to run out on the court for games. I got to travel with the team to tournaments. There was a high school tournament held in Seattle just before Christmas 1989, which is when the "slapping" incident occurred.

Most of the guys on our team were players and they were "playas". I was one of only three white guys on the team – which I was always completely comfortable with, but these guys were studs of the highest order that never had trouble getting girls and I was thoroughly shy with the ladies. The first night in Seattle, there were 10 of us in one room. It was late, the lights were off, and they all started talking about jerking off. The guys told me this was a team ritual, one that they did annually to encourage "bonding" – brought the team together. So, in complete darkness, I hear the sound of pants being pulled down, groans and grunts, and the unmistakable sound of slapping hand to skin repeatedly. Well, I thought to myself, I'm not going to be the only one not spanking the monkey, so let's do this! Now I'm yankin' the sausage, kinda groaning to myself, and then...the lights go up. I'm the only one with my pants down. Every one of these fuckers had mimicked the sound of pulling the love chain by slapping their hands on their arms and were laughing at me. Which, you would think, would be the worst part...but it wasn't.

When we got back to San Francisco, every single student at the school knew what happened. I mean everyone (and this was way before social media or even the internet!!). I was the kid that everyone did a double-take on as I walked down the hallway. It was a veritable rubbernecking, like a freak show or a six-car pileup on the 101.

But that wasn't the worst part.

The worst part was my Journalism teacher, who said to me as I walked out of his class that afternoon, "So Jeremy...spankin' in Seattle, huh?"

You might think I would have considered dropping out, or changing schools, or even committing suicide after such a horrible public humiliation. Yet somehow, I just kept on truckin' at that school. In fact, I became the President of our chapter of the California Scholarship Federation, and was the first to walk out and represent our class at graduation. How was I able to shake off such a terrible event? Maybe it was because I was going to Madonna and Paul McCartney concerts and having conversations with Paula Abdul and they weren't.

CHAPTER 6

"CONVENTION"AL WISDOM

It was at an industry convention that I watched Duran Duran play a private show at the Playboy Mansion while I was having a conversation with the Barenaked Ladies (the band. And you may be surprised that there were no bare naked ladies). It was at an industry convention that I sang lead vocals for an industry band at the legendary Tipitina's in New Orleans following a performance by Nawlins legends The Iguanas. It was at an industry convention that I met Ozzy Osbourne with my mother. It was at an industry convention that I had lunch with Ringo Starr.

It was as simple as a record rep noticing me coming out of a session and asking, "Wanna have lunch with Ringo Starr?" Goosebumps. Literal goosebumps all over my arms because yes, that was in fact "Sgt. Pepper's Lonely Hearts Club Band" that I used to spin on my record player every night when I went to sleep from the age of 2. It was a pretty sweet record player, too – there was a little notch that you pressed in that allowed for the record to flip itself when one side had completed. The music never stopped all night long. Sgt. Pepper's and "Abbey Road" were my favorites when it came to The Beatles, and they sat on the nightstand next to the double album "Goodbye Yellow Brick Road" by Elton John, "Bridge Over Troubled Water" by Simon & Garfunkel, and "Free To Be You And Me" by Marlo Thomas. It was as if my mother decided I was going to grow up with serious musical cred on the playground, but the throw-in of the Marlo Thomas acknowledged that I wasn't even potty trained.

The lunch with Ringo was in a dimly lit private room with

about 20 people around a long table. Ringo and his wife Barbara Bach sat at the head of the table and predictably, all the yahoos from other radio stations got up in Ringo's business before he even had a chance to order a salad. I, on the other hand, was biding my time, plotting my moment. Yes, it would have been more exciting - ne, I would have nearly thrown up on myself had Paul McCartney been the one sitting there. But ladies and gentlemen, I was having lunch with a Beatle. A BEATLE!!! By this time in my life (I was in my late 20s), I had met many rock stars and usually it was no big deal, and sometimes I didn't say anything. This one I didn't want to screw up. I wanted to say exactly the right thing at exactly the right moment and wanted to remember it that way for the rest of my life.

That moment came at the "intermission" of the meal, between the salad and the main course. I recognized Ringo was alone for the first time at the end of the table, and most of the others were talking to each other or in the bathroom. I quietly slinked down to Ringo, knelt down next to him, and said, "Ringo, I just want you to know that the music of The Beatles meant everything to me. It shaped my taste in music, it was the guiding factor in my career choice, and the fact that I'm able to tell you this in person means the world to me." (How many times do I think I practiced that during the Salmon Bruchetta)? Ringo took a long look at me, then said, "What's your favorite Beatles album?" Not missing a beat, I replied, "Sgt. Peppers". Again, with no pause, Ringo wants to know, "And what's your favorite song on that album?" It should be noted that my favorite song on that album is "A Day in the Life", the haunting tale at the end of the LP about the lucky man who made the grade. But that's not what I said. My ultra-fast response was "With A Little Help From My Friends". I know enough about Ringo to know that not only does he sing on that track, he's always treated it as his magnum opus. Well, you should have seen him after that. "That's my mate!", Ringo spouted with glee. He stood up, put his arm around me, and called the photographer over. The picture taken at exactly that moment sits on the mantle above the fireplace.

The very first convention I attended was The Gavin Convention in San Francisco in 1990. Music industry conventions these days can be a shell of their former selves. I remember when Seagram bought MCA Records in 1995, because that marked a moment in time when corporations were buying record labels solely focused on the bottom line. That started a sea change on the record side. There's no doubt that conventions in the 70's and early 80's must have been really something. But in 1990, you could still find record label suites with top shelf open bars, pinball machines, and topless women.

At only 17 years old, I was in the X100 suite for the Gavin Convention on a February Friday night. Jane Child had a #1 single on the radio called "Don't Want to Fall In Love", and she was sitting on my lap. The DJs were broadcasting live from the suite, and I could not believe my good fortune. I desperately wanted to go into the record label suites, but I didn't have a pass for that. I noticed that there were two methods of admission for the parties – you either had a badge or a wristband. Someone next to me had one of the wristbands and I was able to get a pretty good look. It looked just like one of those wristbands they give you when you're admitted at the hospital. That observation led to perhaps my most creative and ballsy venture.

The next day, I called up my friend Mark and informed him of my discovery. I cooked up a plan for us to drive around to San Francisco hospitals. We would tell the nurse that we were high school drama students doing a school play and we needed two wristbands for the performance. Every single nurse said "no problem" and went to get us a couple of wristbands. We needed a certain color, however – red. The first wristbands were white, no good. The second hospital's bands were orange and the shape was awkward – not a good match. When the nurse at the third hospital emerged holding two red wristbands, we didn't believe it. They looked absolutely identical to the band I saw the previous night at the convention. Although I'm sure there were intrinsic differences like the number of holes or the exact shape of the spot where you insert the name of the patient, I was certain there was no chance that a security guard would notice. I was right. That's the story of how two 17-year olds crashed every record label party at the Gavin Convention in 1990. Free drinks, free looks at boobies, and one hell of a night.

I recall meeting Paula Abdul at that convention but I spoke to her on the phone before then. X100 hired a night guy named "Supersnake" and they came up with a stunt for his first night. Paula had a hit song at the time called "Cold Hearted", the lyrics of which went "He's a cold hearted snake, look into his eyes. Uh-oh, he's been tellin' lies". So, "Cold Hearted Snake", "Supersnake", you get the idea. Snake "locked" himself in the studio, taking the station "hostage" by playing "Cold Hearted" over and over and over again. It had the desired effect – people freaked out, flooding the phone lines, which were being answered by yours truly. These listeners were expressing genuine concern that the station was in trouble, being overtaken by some lunatic named Supersnake. One of the callers said to me, "Hi, this is Paula Abdul. Why are you playing my song over and over?" I berated her a bit, thinking there was no way in hell that Paula Abdul was actually calling a radio station, but I eventually played along. "It's terrible, Paula. This guy calling himself Supersnake has locked himself in our studio and he keeps playing your song and refuses to come out. "That's awful", the woman said. "I hope everything works out ok." I hung up, not thinking much more of it. 15 minutes later, the fire department showed up, followed by the police (much to the great joy of the programming department – it doesn't occur to radio people that a stunt might be affecting the proper use of our city's emergency services). They banged on the door, and of course we let them in, relented, and the stunt dissipated soon after. Was Paula the one who called the cops? We'll never know....

CHAPTER 7

SHAKE, RATTLE, ROCK AND ROLL

October 17th, 1989 at 5:07pm was the most eventful day of my internship as that was the day San Francisco was hit with a 7.1 magnitude earthquake. As a child of the Bay Area, I had been through my share of quakes. Earthquake drills in grade school were as common as fire drills. We knew that you could get under a desk or a table, so that you weren't hit by flying debris. You could position yourself in a doorway, in case the structure were to collapse around you. If you were indoors when the quake began, you should stay indoors and if you were outside, stay outside.

When the 1989 earthquake struck, I was at my post answering the request lines for Chuck Geiger during the afternoon show on the other side of the glass partition that separated producer from DJ. The Bay Area was enraptured by what was being referred to as the "Bay Bridge Series", the World Series between the San Francisco Giants and the Oakland Athletics. I had a TV positioned on one of those carts upon which teachers used to set their 16 millimeter projector for class presentations – like "Red Asphalt" in drivers training. When the shaking began, I had just hung up the phone with a listener who had requested Madonna's "Vogue", and the song playing on the station was a ballad called "Angelia" by Richard Marx.

The next 30 seconds or so felt like an eternity – like the effect they use regularly in "Inception" that slows down the action. The song seemed to decline into a very.......slow....and.....low....pitched....speed. As I dove under the console (as I was taught in all those drills, of course), I watched the JBL speakers hanging from the wall swing back and forth, crashing against the massive glass windows that overlooked the downtown skyscrapers. I observed some buildings swaying and others shaking violently (depending on its age and whether or not it had been retrofitted to current earthquake standards). As we were on the 7th floor of the building and it was a more recently built structure, it did what it was supposed to do – swaying with the movement of the ground. That meant as it swung side to side, I found myself alternating between crawling up the floor and trying to keep myself from sliding down the floor. I remember screaming out, "We're going to die!!!" – which wasn't particularly heroic or helpful for the moment, though I'm fairly certain nobody heard the death knell through the solid soundproof studio door.

That was the true indicator about how obvious it was that this earthquake was much worse than anything we'd experienced before. It seemed like even quakes in the 5.0-6.0 range had happened every few years, but this felt immediately like the big one. When it stopped, we were off the air but not for very long. It would turn out that we were the only FM station whose generator kept us running.

The first inclination of the higher ups was to give away "Earthquake Survival Kits" – but it was really more of a topical joke than a practical kit. In the era before cell phones and internet, we had no way of knowing how bad the damage was. We had two sources of news at that time – the AP news wire, which was disabled by the quake, and TV news. We were all standing around watching KPIX news show the first pictures of the Bay Bridge collapse. We saw that horrible footage of the car that plummeted down that portion of the bridge. Then we saw the images of the double deck Nimitz Freeway in Oakland, which folded on top of itself like dominoes. Then we saw the crack in Candlestick Park, where the World Series was being played. That's when it became apparent playing commercial-free sweeps of Janet Jackson and New Kids on the Block would not be the order of the day.

The morning team was summoned back to the station to host programming on the station until further notice. Anyone working at the station was asked to help out in any way possible – much of which involved gathering news from the TV (and the news wire, once it started back up) and bringing the information to the hosts. The morning team ended up doing a remarkable job that day, doing what great radio stations do during times of crisis. They became a sounding board for the community – alternating between offering the latest news and information, letting listeners vent about how the earthquake was affecting them, and requesting songs that were appropriate for the emotions of the moment. I stayed at the station until about 12:30am that night, and had never felt a greater sense of gratification. I was helpful, felt like I performed a real public service, while at the same time feeling the vibe of community around me. The people working at the radio station felt like my brothers and sisters and the events of that day further invigorated and inspired my love of the drug that is radio.

CHAPTER 8

A BINKY, 100,000 WATTS AND ONE TOO MANY MAI TAIS

"Binky" was the name given to the head of the Research department at X100, whose responsibilities included a weekend shift from 2am-6am. One Friday night, there was a station remote at a nightclub near Fisherman's Wharf, and as usual I found my underage self at the party – though I wasn't drinking that night. Most of the staff was there that night, including a couple of our prime time DJs. Binky was rocking the Mai Tais to the point of no return on an empty stomach and it wasn't until about 12:30am that someone realized that the Bink was in no shape to perform his duties. So, everyone (including the DJs, two promotions staffers, me, and Binky) packed into the station Suburban and headed back to the station.

The station was a two level operation, with sales on the lower floor and programming upstairs. You took the elevator to the first level of the station, on which you'd find the lobby and a couch to the right. Binky waddled back and forth like a penguin – a very inebriated penguin until his knees hit the sofa and he fell face first into the furniture. It was approximately 1am.

Upon this development, a pow-wow took place on the upper level with all of us in attendance. It became quickly apparent that neither of the two DJs had any interest in sticking around and covering Binky's ass, and they left shortly thereafter. With less than an hour to go before airtime, only me and the two promotions employees were left to come up with a plan, which we did. Since I'd been running the console

31

on the weekends for syndicated shows such as the Rick Dees and Casey Kasem countdown shows, I knew how to operate the equipment. I walked downstairs to the couch to fetch the stinky Binky, who we literally had to carry on our shoulders up the stairs into the studio where I positioned him near the microphone.

I turned on the reel-to-reel machine (there was no digital recording in the studio in 1989) and grabbed some of the liner cards that were resting on the glass shelf above the console. Liner cards were statements that Program Directors made for the DJs to read verbatim. Things like "X100 – The Outrageous FM" or "You're listening to 99 minutes of music in a row on X100" or "Kelly and Kline in the Morning, the most hits all day- X100!" I figured that if I could record Bink voicing some of these liners, I could simply play them over music for the next few hours while he lay passed out. Hopefully, the Program Director (who listened ALL the time and wasn't shy about hotlining the air talent – more on that later) wouldn't notice. It should be noted that I edited some of his breaks together using chalk, tape, and razor blades – this was the archaic stone-age way of editing that thankfully was replaced with one computer button touch cutting and pasting with digital technology.

There Bink was, in all his drunken splendor, propped up against the tape machine. There was me, angling the microphone just right, so I could capture the moment. Behind me were the two trusty promotions girls, loyally sticking around to help. I pressed "record" on the player, held Binky up with one hand, and presented the yellow liner cards with black sharpie in my other hand. It was on. Liner #1. "X100...The Out....(super fast) rageousFM!" Oh boy. There was definitely a little slurring and the enunciating and pacing was terrible. This plan will never work. Binky is surely going to get fired. Well, what do we have to lose. Let's do another one. Bink, balanced – card, up. "X100 – Hits Happen at ninety nine point seven F-M". Huh! That one wasn't half bad! Not good, but serviceable. We continued this exercise with five more cards until it seemed Bink had reached his limit. "Let's get him back to an office", I said.

The three of us carried him back to an office on the upper floor at around 1:30am, where he passed out again on a different sofa. At 2:10am, the grand experiment began as I played the recording of the first liner over Milli Vanill's "Girl You Know It's True". (Perhaps ironic that I was faking "live Binky" while playing a band that would later be busted for lip-syncing). Hit button to trigger song, hit other button to trigger playing of tape machine with levels slightly higher. Watch phone carefully to see if the hotline rings. No ring. The exercise will continue. And continue it did, for the next two hours with no problems whatsoever. That is, until we decided there was a risk in repeating too many of the same liners. Surely if we did that, it would get noticed. Instead, we would go fetch Binky from his second passed out stage of the night, bring him back in the studio, and record a new batch of liners to get us through the Rick Dees countdown at 6. This would be a very bad decision.

We carried Binky back into the studio on our shoulders, as before and prepared to restart the process with a new batch of liners. Reel-to-reel ready? Check. Binky ready? Check. Liner cards in hand? Check. Hit record. Ok, Bink, 3-2-1, and...go. "X100, TheOutrage.......OUUUUAHHHHHHHHCHHHAHHH." I'm not sure how to spell the sound of vomit, but that's about what it sounded like. The other noise in the room was the piercing scream coming from me and the two promotions employees. As for what it looked like, well, you've seen barf before. But I'll bet you haven't seen it covering a radio station control board. Fact of the matter is, we were very lucky with the yacking incident. The vast majority of the vomit landed on the floor – most of the stuff that came close to the board covered the edge on the panel that framed the console, and only a little got on the buttons. I've seen someone spill coffee on a board before and exactly what you think would happen, happens. Sparks fly, circuits short out, and the radio station goes off the air. Once when this happened at my station in Syracuse, the engineers had to set up a satellite studio in another room for days until they could repair the main console. In this case, the amazing promotions girls (who were still there at the station for support) found as many strong cleaners and chemicals as they could find and went to work. They sponged and scrubbed, scrubbed and sponged. They sprayed air freshener and did everything they could to ensure that nobody would know what happened. There were no windows that opened in the studio, which would make scent elimination a particularly challenging task. At 5:30am, Bink woke up, thanked us and apologized, and left the building. At 6am, the shift turned over to the countdown which conveniently I was running anyway- so there was no one that we had to explain his absence to. In fact, all signs pointed to us getting away with it, until....

Monday afternoon, when I was producing the afternoon show and I was telling the story to afternoon host Chuck Geiger. Come on, I had to tell him the story. First of all, he was there that night (until he left me in the lurch), so he was dying to know what transpired and I, frankly, wanted credit for my heroic actions. I had just about finished telling the tale, when I got to the climax with the golden line, "and then he threw up on the board." Pause. Response. "HE THREW UP ON THE BOARD??" Voice from outside the door – "Who threw up on the board?" Oh my god. The studio door was open. Of all people that heard that line, it had to be the Chief

Engineer.

So yeah, the Chief Engineer told the Program Director and the Program Director had a little chat with the Bink. But he didn't fire him and my adventure became the stuff of radio lore. Naturally, all the jocks thought I should have taken the opportunity to crack the mic while I had the chance but I'm glad I didn't. For starters, I wasn't ready to go on the air. But mostly, my actions that night were the driving force behind the best decisions I would make my entire life – thinking about others before myself. There were times that I was an incredibly self-centered teenager. I am proud to say this was not one of those times. A few years later during college, I took a paid summer internship at KFRC, where Bink was now working - so it would be a second tour of duty together. He took the opportunity to tell me how much that night meant to him and how thankful he was. We remain friends to this day.

CHAPTER 9

THAT WAS #25 ON THE COUNTDOWN.
THE TOP 10 IS NEXT!!!

The Program Director of X100 may not have called the hotline the night of the Binky affair, but he sure lit it up one morning that I was running "Rick Dees Weekly Top 40".

I was attending a house party with many X100 staff and I'm sure I got no more than 3 hours of sleep that night. In retrospect, it is one of those nights you're just thankful that the alarm clock worked. I showed up for my shift at 6am that Sunday morning, ready to run the countdown, which at the time was delivered to the station on <u>vinyl</u>. It's not that there weren't CDs in 1990 – there were – but many radio stations at the time were still running most of their music, commercials and other elements on "carts" – clunky cartridges that looked like 8-track tapes. Since we weren't equipped with CD players yet, syndicated shows were still delivered on satellite or on records.

Playing a countdown on two record players shouldn't be too complicated. You put the first side on one of the turntables, "slip cue" the needle (slide the record back a quarter turn so it starts perfectly on the air) and let it play. When the side is over, you go to local commercials. When the commercials are over, you go to the next side on the other turntable. Which is all well and good except that the back side of "Side 1", I believe, was "Side 6". The back of "Side 2" was "Side 7". So you could understand, couldn't you, how someone could accidentally go from Side 3 to side 9 (instead of side 4) because he put the wrong side of the record on the turntable? So Dees went into the commercial break from #25 and back in the countdown with #10? You could see that innocent mistake happening, right?

It happened and the hotline rang and the Program Director gave me an earful.

CHAPTER 10

JEWISH GUILT AND THE FAKE ID

I was so awkward when I got to Syracuse University to begin my freshman year in the fall of 1990. Radio had a profound social impact on my life, in that I had spent the past couple of years hanging out with people that were older than me and that made me comfortable. When I was hanging out with people that were my age and those not involved in radio, I felt like a fish out of water. I knew two things upon my arrival at Sadler Hall (my dorm, which was located right across the road from the Carrier Dome). I wanted to have sex (hadn't done that yet) and I wanted to drink beer.

It didn't take too long for the beer part...it was the first night. "We three geeks" that met in the hallway of the dorm on the first day devised a plan to get beer. We walked down to Marshall Street (nicknamed M street, the main drag on the campus of Syracuse where the bars and restaurants are) and planted ourselves outside the convenience store, where we waited to ask someone that was old enough to purchase beer for us. Incredibly, our plan worked, and we toted our newly acquired 12 pack of Miller Lite cans back to the dorm carefully in the bag so nobody could see it.

That night, after the sky turned pitch black, we walked up the hill behind Sadler, had a seat on the grass under the stars, and cracked open our brewskies. Ah, this was freedom. We were men now. We...had a flashlight shining in our faces. "What are you boys doing?", said the officer – who wasn't actually a police officer but a Syracuse University campus security guard. "We...were just enjoying a beer on this beautiful night, sir.", I said. For some reason I became the spokesperson for the group. "Can I see your ID?", he asked. The other two guys handed them their driver license and I, too, handed them a form of identification but it wasn't exactly "official".

Back in San Francisco, there were places where you could get an ID for about ten bucks. They took your photo, put it on this laminated card that looked like a driver license, and it said "California" on it, but anyone that would mistake this for a legal form of ID would have to have some form of mental deficiency. It was cheap and an obvious fraud. Today, McLovin would have this ID in his wallet. This was the ID I handed the guard.

He looked at it carefully, turned it around (it was blank on the back!), and before he could say anything, I blurted out, "It's a fake! I don't want it anymore! I'm sorry, here's the real one. I don't know why I gave that to you right now. Please take it. Just take it. I'm sorry".

He looked at our actual pieces of identification and (like he didn't know already) noticed that we were all well under the legal drinking age of 21. He said, "I could call your parents, you know", as he watched the horrified looks on our faces. Pause. "But I'm not going to." What? "You're not allowed to have open containers. Go back to your dorm and don't let me catch you doing this again."

Whew.

CHAPTER 11

LUCKY I DIDN'T END UP *IN* AN ALABAMA SLAMMER

Unlike my completely awkward and transitional freshman year at Syracuse University, I came out guns blazing full of confidence right out of the sophomore year gate. About a month into the fall semester, I was already dating, I had a prime shift at the college radio station, and on one fateful Saturday night these things converged into one bad idea.

Z89 operates in many ways like any commercial radio station. It is not your mom's college radio station. Built to mirror what radio professionals will experience in the "real world", it is formatted with a tight Top 40 playlist. We had a research staff, production wizards, and some absurdly talented DJs. This is going to sound nuts, but during the time I was at Z89, the 100,000 watt commercial Top 40 station in Syracuse would run pieces of imaging attacking Z89. Can you imagine a commercial radio station feeling threatened by a college station? (We may have goaded them on.) Some of the finest media talent in the country today can proudly claim Z89 on their resume. We had a sales team, and hosted events around the community. Despite the fact that it was run by college kids, this included bar nights. As many of our listeners were not students, these bars were occasionally off-campus. This led me, my new girlfriend, and most of the station staff to an off-campus establishment that didn't seem to have much of a problem serving minors. I'm not sure if it was because it was the special of the night. It may have been because some others were drinking it. Or maybe I'd heard of the concoction and figured I'd try one. Whatever the reason, I started downing Alabama Slammers.

The Alabama Slammer is comprised of Amaretto, Southern Comfort, Sloe Gin, and Orange Juice and is served in a tall glass. The three liquors are far more prominent in the drink than the OJ. I didn't have one, not two, not three...but six Alabama Slammers. This was the first time in my life I blacked out for periods and have no memory for blocks of time. I remember that we ended up at Lambda Chi Alpha, a fraternity to which one of the station DJs belonged. I remember feeling very sick. I remember thinking I was going to die. I remember someone calling an ambulance. I remember sitting on the edge of the ambulance and declining treatment because I realized I was going to be ok – I was just hammered beyond belief and beyond any point I had ever experienced.

I remember, despite the embarrassment of this happening in the Lambda Chi house in front of the brothers, returning to the scene just days later during fraternity rush week. I remember being asked questions during the interview portion. I remember one of the questions was, "What's your favorite college mascot?" I remember my response was the South Carolina Gamecocks, and I remember them asking me why I chose the Gamecocks. I remember my reply was "Because I like cocks". I remember never setting foot in Lambda Chi Alpha again.

The most surprising part of that story is that the girl I went on a date with that night turned into a long term relationship that lasted through junior year.

But really, who wouldn't want a piece of *that*??

CHAPTER 12

THAT GUY IS A RIOT

The sure fire way to get into bars and get free drinks as a college sophomore is to get a job DJing at a college bar. Word got around that 44's (named after the heralded number worn by legends like Jim Brown and Ernie Davis at Syracuse) was looking for a DJ and I needed some money. My first night on the job was on something called "OV Split Day". OV, or Old Vienna beer, was a Midwestern and now Canadian produced beer that, for a time, offered their product up in 7 ounce bottles. On OV Split Day at 44's, you could get a bucket of them for five dollars. OV Split Day started around 7am (44's was a true remnant of the late 80's, when Syracuse was regularly on the top of Playboy's "Top Party Schools in America" rankings). You can imagine, then, what it was like in there when I showed up for my very first shift at 9pm on OV Split Day. Just like the scene in "Animal House", glass bottles were being thrown across the bar, hitting the wall or smashing on the floor. The levels of intoxication were like nothing I've ever seen. Some jackass upperclassmen tried to stop me from getting to the DJ booth, but I squirmed my way there and started setting up.

Soon thereafter, the owner of the bar stopped in to the booth and asked me to play a mid-tempo Bob Seger song. "Sure", I said. "I'll try to get to it." I was a college sophomore and I was already using classic radio DJ lingo on my boss like he was calling the request line. We have lots of stock answers when someone calls the radio station request line. "I'll try to get to it" is one. "I'll see what I can do" has got to be #1. "Sure, it's coming up" was used with regularity because DJs figure it's always coming up. Might not be coming up for three days, but it's coming up. I was exhibiting an inordinate level of cockiness for a sophomore and I had no intention of playing a midtempo Bob Seger track on OV Split Day.

The first couple of hours of my shift went fine as I blended classic rock with newer material. Some dance stuff, vintage bar rock like The Doors – everyone was happy. Then, right around 11pm on OV Split Day, I played "Bring The Noise" by Public Enemy and Anthrax. The place went apeshit. I mean, people were jumping up and down, spilling their beers, and running into each other on purpose as if they were in a mosh pit. 44's became one giant messy smelly drunken mosh pit. We were in the lower bar and you could hear some rumblings (more like screaming) of something awry in the upper bar. The next thing I knew, the police were on the scene and we heard, "Bar's closed! Everybody out!" As the entire bar was cleared out, it became apparent that I had started a riot. A full on swingfest broken up by mace, was the word on the street. I was certain that the owner would fire me for playing "Bring the Noise" and shutting down his bar three hours early on one of his busiest days of the year. I wouldn't have been surprised if he fired me for neglecting to play his Bob Seger request. But he didn't fire me. I worked there for a few more months, got a lot of free drinks, and made $75 cash each time I worked. Not such a bad deal for a sophomore.

CHAPTER 13

LAST NIGHT IN EUROPE

How awesome is my mother? When I was about to finish my sixth and final week of my summer studying Spanish in Spain and was preparing to come home, my mom said, "This is an opportunity you may never have again. You need to stay in Europe." So I did.

I traveled with one of the guys on my Study Abroad program from Spain to London, where we made our way to Soho. Whereas I was pining to go to Abbey Road to see where the Beatles recorded, my traveling companion was intent on going to a strip club in Soho – and so we did. Strip clubs in London use the same tricks similar establishments use in America – girls come up to you and ask you to buy them a drink. If you're not well versed in this area you say "sure" and you find out an hour later that you've been buying $75 drinks and that will be $300 please. Neither I, nor my friend was carrying that sort of money and, as a result of their threats of – well, I don't even know what they were threatening to do but it must have been very intimidating - we were foolish enough to go to an ATM, come back and give them the cash. The show itself was a "live sex show" in which the participants didn't actually have sex. It was simulated sex, interactive with the audience. "Would you like me to do it haaarder, or should I do it softer?" It was pathetic, sad, and embarrassing that we had given them all that money. It was a mistake that would cost me at the end of this trip – more on that later. While in London, I connected with the girlfriend of one of my best friends at Syracuse. She was studying in France and wanted me to come to Paris for Bastille Day. After our strip club fiasco in London, we were ready for a switch so we took the boat to

Paris for Bastille Day celebrations.

My stay in Paris was a blast, even though I was staying in a very cheap, run down hostel . After the strip club faux pas and the purchase of a ticket to Les Miserables in London (worth every penny), my finances were running very low. I met a fellow American at the hostel and on the afternoon before I was scheduled to fly home, he asked me if I wanted to hit the town. We started by heading for the subway station and, while waiting for the train, I was approached by a gentleman that blurted something out in French. "No parlez vous frances", I responded. Sometimes, since Americans aren't generally well treated in France, I would offer to speak Spanish . I found the French sometimes preferred to speak Spanish over English. The response to my response, however, was "Oh, you speak English?" "I do", I replied, and discovered that this guy was from Los Angeles and was in Paris with his two cousins. His two very attractive cousins who also happened to be standing on the subway platform. "What are you guys doing tonight?", he asked, and truth be told we had no plans. We were just headed out for a night on the town. "Would you like to join us?", I was asked. The obvious answer was yes, and the evening was underway.

First stop was dinner, and it was a glorious summer night in Paris. In a restaurant close to the Seine with sidewalk seating, we spent hours enjoying dinner, many bottles of wine, and cigarettes. I don't smoke (and in fact I can't stand cigarettes), but after a generous amount of alcohol and the good company, I very well may have smoked an entire pack myself at dinner. Following our eating excursion, we headed to a club called Rue St Germain that one of us had seen in a travel guide. It was one of those clubs where they look at you through a small sliding door and decide whether or not you are privileged enough to grace their presence. We apparently fit the bill as the door opened, and we were escorted downstairs into what was known as the St. Germain's Opium Lounge.

The Opium Lounge was funky as any entertainment venue I've ever seen. Dimly lit with lava lamps, orange and red hues and bean bags on the floor for seating arrangements, the lounge was packed and we grabbed the last 7 bags which were in the front row. In front of us, a French band was playing American music in a thick accent and we were absolutely loving it. I knew I was getting perilously low on money by this point, but I wasn't going to let anything ruin this evening so when the waitress asked me what I wanted to drink, I said, "Whatever you recommend". Her recommendation (which, of course, she just brought me) was Framboise Lambic – a very tasty raspberry tinged beer that went down smoother than a beer should, so naturally I ordered 3 of them over the course of the night. It wasn't until the check came later that I learned the Framboise Lambic was $45. Each.

We're just having a grand time when the band breaks into "Give Me The Night" by George Benson which is especially amusing when sung in the French accent. "So gimme the night", he wails. Then firmly and stiffly, "All right, All right". As I'm apt to do in times like this, I was singing along which may have normally gone unnoticed except for the fact that the seven loud Americans were in their bean bags in the front row. The music stopped and the lead singer pointed at me. "You", he said. "You want to sing with us?" The crowd of mostly French cheered, encouraging me on. I didn't need any encouraging. "Yeah", I said, and hopped up on the stage to the delight of the crowd. The band conferred amongst themselves for a moment, and then I asked, "What do you want me to sing?" "Elvis Presley", was the response. "No problem", I confidently assured them.

"Don't Be Cruel" was the selection, and I killed it. Complete with swiveling hips and twirling of the microphone, I had the crowd in my hands and I was completely in my element. When the last guitar lick played, I said – naturally - "Thank you. Thank you very much" and hopped off the stage back to my group. I was getting a standing ovation and felt so incredibly high, the $150 bill for my beer barely bothered me. The problem was, even though it was 2:30 in the morning, the night wasn't over – and I was broke. Oh, and my flight back to the United States was at Noon.

This is the part of the night where I blacked out. Not completely blacked out – like don't remember anything – but blacked out like you remember things in 10 minute increments spread 45 minutes apart. I remember being in line at a discoteque with the same group of people. There was a bouncer taking a $20 cover charge at the door, and I certainly remember saying to my posse that I had no money to get in. None of them could really spare an extra $20 and still afford to drink inside, so I was fairly certain the night was to end there...except my next memory is of being inside this club and dancing very intimately with one of the girls from L.A. We were on the dance floor talking about Lenny Kravitz, because I must have told her how I had seen Robert Plant opening for Lenny Kravitz in Madrid (I know that in itself sounds very strange). It was at that point that one of Lenny's very early songs, "Mr. Cab Driver", came on and we were dancing with delight until someone walked onto the dance floor and handed me a drink. I looked at him and asked, "Where did this come from?" His response, as he pointed in the direction of a booth at the corner of the disco with a soft glowing light – "She bought it for you."

"She" was drop dead stunning. I'm not kidding, one of the most beautiful women I've ever seen. So beautiful, in fact, that

I ditched the girl from Los Angeles – literally walked off the dance floor without saying a word – and made my way to the booth at the corner of the disco with the soft glowing light. "I understand you bought this for me.", I said. "I saw you sing tonight at the St. Germain", she replied. I sat down next to my new biggest only fan in Paris. Introductions lead me to discover that my fan was a South African model. Seriously. She was by herself and we had a delightful time (though I felt bad later about ditching my group). We even hit one more bar at 5am – a reggae bar that featured a drink called "Vuelva a la Vida". Knowing this meant "Return to Life" in espanol and since I was fading fast and needed a pick me up seeing that my flight was in seven hours, I ordered said drink without inquiring about its ingredients. The bartender reached under the bar and pulled out one giant bottle of Absolut Vodka and slammed it in front of me. He reached down again and appeared with a giant bottle of hot sauce, which he proceeded to place next to the bottle of vodka. The bottles were soon accompanied by two shot glasses. He poured a shot of vodka in one of them, and a shot of hot sauce in the other. Lechaim! My new lady friend must have paid for this drink, because I had not acquired any new wealth between 230 and 5am. As Vuelva a La Vida didn't come with an instruction manual, I elected to make the hot sauce the first shot and the vodka the chaser. The effect of this concoction was absolutely as advertised, and I was feeling newly energized. We danced to the sounds of Bob Marley, Peter Tosh, and Jimmy Cliff for the next 75 minutes, when it was getting close to the time the subway (which was basically free in Paris – even the guide book said to jump the turnstiles) would open and I could make my way home.

Upon my arrival at the hotel, the front desk clerk confirmed that I was leaving that day, to which I indeed validated. Since it was 7:30 at this point, all I had time for was packing, a shower, and then get to the airport with some time to spare. I figured I would sleep on the plane but unfortunately my body had other ideas. I fell asleep.

The phone rang. "Aren't you checking out today, Mr. Nachlis?", said the voice. "What time is it?", I asked. "10:30", he replied. 30 minutes past check out time. "Shit! I'll be right down." In 10 minutes, I threw all my clothes and assorted items haphazardly into my suitcase. No time for a shower, I bolted downstairs and checked out as quickly as I could. Though I didn't have enough money for a taxi to the airport, I did have the required ten dollars for a bus ride to Charles De Gaulle International. The bus, which operated every hour on the hour, was about a 15 minute walk away so I ran with my suitcase swinging from side to side down one block after another. The bus was there and I made it with only 5 minutes to spare. It was a 40 minute bus ride to the airport and at 11:42am I made my way to the TWA counter and announced my arrival. "I'm here for my flight!" The attendant took my ticket and passport. Click-click-click-click-clickety click on the computer. "You missed your flight, sir.", I was told. "What? No, it's 11:45, my flight is at noon, I can make it!", I said as-a-matter-of-factly. "Sir", she calmly explained, "Although the aircraft is still at the gate, it is scheduled to leave on time. You have an international flight and you will not get through security on time. I'm sorry."

I was impossibly dejected. "My grandparents are waiting for me in New York", I told her. "I don't know how I'm going to explain this to them. I've been in Europe studying for school for two months and I'm out of money. I can't even afford to spend one more night in Paris." She looked me up and down and said, "Let me see what I can do." Click-click-click-click-clickety-click. "There is one more flight today and it leaves at 2pm.", she said. Well, this was great news! I could just tell my grandparents that I got bumped from the Noon flight and would be in a couple hours later. No big deal. Happens all the time. "Unfortunately, Mr. Nachlis, coach is full." I don't remember what I did when she told me that. I may have given her puppy dog eyes. It's possible I hung my head low in utter depression and loss. It is even entirely possible that tears filled the eyes. What is certain is I did something, and that something worked. "It's your lucky day", she told me. "I'm going to upgrade you to business class." After a thousand thank yous for the attendant, I walked over to a pay phone where I made a collect call ("dial 10-10-321, then the number!") to my grandparents. The story worked like a charm, and I would arrive a mere two hours after the original time. The next big decision? I hadn't showered, I smelled like a carton of cigarettes, and frankly I wasn't just hungover, I was still a little drunk. But I knew what business class meant. Free drinks. Hair of the dog, people. Hair of the dog. God bless my grandparents. When I arrived in New York, although I stunk to high heaven and looked like hell, they gave me a hug and a kiss and never said anything but "We love you and missed you".

CHAPTER 14

I SAW STARS ON OUR FIRST DATE

Technically, the Saturday afternoon trip to Song Mountain in Tully, NY near Syracuse was not the first date for me and my wife. We met at a sorority party in a bar called Darwin's on M Street and our first date was with friends at Chuck's, the finest dark, dingy, Grateful Dead-playing campus bar there's ever been. But our first real "date" alone with no accompaniment was a day ski trip.

I had done some cross-country skiing when I was younger but I was an extreme novice when it came to downhill activities. I'm even fairly certain that the first time I got on the ski lift that day was the first time I had ever gotten on one. That would explain why, when we were next in line to get on the lift to take us up on the mountain, I awkwardly ambled on my skis to the line where you stand to get on the lift. It would certainly explain why I wasn't standing in the proper position on the line and was not paying attention when the large bar in the middle that connects the lift to the cable above knocked me squarely on the side of my head. I wasn't knocked out but, as I slumped in the lift just a bit as it began its ascent up the mountain, I was certainly woozy and my eyes blinked rapidly as I attempted to get my bearings. Jennifer asked, "Are you ok?" and my stoic first date reply, of course, was "Oh, I'm fine." I couldn't take back the humiliating faux pas of the lift-head collision, but surely I could get some of my pride back by skiing like a champ.

As the lift made its way to the summit, the temperature grew colder and colder and effectively numbed my pain. This feeling allowed me to ski for the next 90 minutes until we were ready to wrap it up. We returned our rental equipment to the lodge and made our way to the car where I got behind the wheel and waited a bit as the heat warmed it up. While the numbness subsided as the temperature got warmer, the previous symptoms of dizziness returned. Less than five minutes down the road, I told Jennifer I needed to stop the car. I pulled over, opened the door, leaned out and spit on the ground. The color of the spit was red. Now, in addition to my wooziness and increasingly painful headache, I was spitting blood.

Now my horrified first date companion wasn't sure where to drive me, and I instructed her to go to the health center on campus because that was a free visit and I was worried about using my parent's health insurance. When we arrived at the health center, we got rapid attention thanks to the blood spitting condition but it was those same symptoms that led the on call physician to instruct us to go to the emergency room at the hospital. Once at the hospital, it was Jennifer that called my parents to let them know what was going on – an interesting way for my mother and stepfather to be introduced to my new lady friend.

Once seen by the nurses, I learned that they listened to me every Friday and Saturday night from Midnight to 6am on Y94FM, which incidentally started in an hour and a half. Now that they realized a local celebrity was in their presence (not really, but as long as they thought so), I was getting the finest and most attentive treatment. I was diagnosed with a concussion and told to go home – the only problem being that there was no possible way the station was going to be able to get a substitute for my shift on such short notice. (Yes, in retrospect that call would have been a good one to make oh, I don't know, the moment I spit blood). The difficulty in getting my shift filled was compounded in 1994 by the fact that we didn't have cell phones yet, and reaching the right people wasn't particularly easy. There was no automation to fall back on. I told the doctor that I would have to do my shift, to which he told me that someone would have to stay with me at the station during my entire shift to "observe" me. Not just because I had spit blood earlier in the day, but also because he gave me some medication that had that nagging "drowsiness" side effect. Hmmm...who would that "someone" be?

So it was on my first date with Jennifer that I hit my head on a ski lift, got a concussion, went to the emergency room, and then did my entire overnight shift at the radio station with her observing me. She would be the last girlfriend I'd ever have, and this year we celebrate our 20th wedding anniversary. I figure if she stuck around that night, we can make it through anything.

CHAPTER 15

ALMOST GOT A CORVETTE – DAMN YOU, CELINE

In the mid 90's, there was a contest for radio program directors and music directors called the AIR competition. AIR (Active Industry Research) was a company that was paid by record labels to get opinions from industry influence-makers. The incentive for us to participate was money. Cold hard cash. Each week, we'd review a list of songs and predict how high on the charts it would climb. Top 40, Top 25, Top 10, #1, or "No Chart", of course meaning it wouldn't crack the Top 40.

The points system was based on high risk, high reward. If you picked a song to go number one, for example, and it did, you would be showered with a ton of points. Consequently, you missed out with conservative or incorrect picks. The grand prize was always something incredibly extravagant, and in this case it was a Corvette worth around $60,000.

As we approached the final week of the competition, I was in first place and in truly dramatic fashion, it would all come down to one song. Unfortunately for me the song was "My Heart Will Go On" by Celine Dion, the theme song to what would become the biggest movie in the history of the world ("Titanic"). I had picked the song to go Top 10 and the guy in second place had it penciled in for #1. The song vaulted from #2 to #1 in the final week of the contest and that guy scored a new Corvette. I'm not sure how I would have handled that (there was a cash option) – I was only 24 years old. I'd like to think I would have used that money wisely and maybe wouldn't have accumulated all that debt. Nah, I would have wasted it.

In the mid-2000's, New York Attorney General Elliot Spitzer went after major record labels, including Sony BMG, Warner Music Group, and Universal Music Group. Spitzer accused label executives of providing personal gifts to radio Program Directors in exchange for airplay of the songs they were promoting. This included cash, Sony Playstations, and personal trips. Each of the labels settled for millions of dollars that were directed to non-profit music programs in New York State. Spitzer also went after radio companies. CBS Radio, Clear Channel, Entercom, and Citadel settled for 12.5 million in fines. This also affected certain practices in the record business, including the utilization of independent promoters as middle men.

Amidst this backdrop, and many radio companies forbidding their Program Directors to participate, Active Industry Research shut its doors in 2005. In an unrelated story, the New York Times revealed in 2008 that Spitzer, who was now Governor of New York, was found to have been utilizing an escort service. This led to Spitzer's resignation just seven days later.

CHAPTER 16

SORRY, CAN'T STAY AT THE PLAYBOY MANSION...I'VE GOT A GIG

I often say that I entered the music industry in just the nick of time. It wasn't the drug-laden 70's, but it wasn't the corporate budget-cutting 2000's either. As I came of age in this business in the 1990's, I attended many conventions and artist showcases, and yes...attended a party at the Playboy Mansion in Los Angeles.

I wasn't just *at* the Playboy Mansion. I was hanging out with the Barenaked Ladies watching Duran Duran perform. A surreal moment for sure, but not so big that I didn't have the cajones to leave my wife and my promotions director to go to a band rehearsal for a show the next night at the House of Blues.

Flash back to a couple years earlier, when I was attending a convention and noticed a band playing cover songs in a hotel suite. They needed a singer, I knew most of the songs, and we were off and running. The band was made up of industry types from the radio and records side of the business. Over the course of the next couple years, we would play- but only at conventions, because that was the only time we got to see each other in the same place. At first, we played in the hotels where the conventions were held. Then, as we got bolder, we played a late night gig following New Orleans legends The Iguanas at the one and only Tipitina's in the French Quarter. Finally, we booked a show at the House of Blues in Los Angeles and someone scheduled a rehearsal at a recording studio the same night as the party at the Playboy Mansion.

A limo took us from the party, as I left my wife at the

Playboy Mansion ("Sorry honey, I've got to leave a party at the Playboy Mansion to go sing in a recording studio") to the studio where we jammed for a few hours and I'll never forget that Benny Mardones showed up and complimented me on my singing. Most people will not recognize the name Benny Mardones, but they will recognize his Adult Contemporary staple "Into The Night" (if I could fly, I'd pick you up....) In a dose of small world syndrome, Benny Mardones is Syracuse's adopted musical son. To this day, Benny will announce a show in Syracuse, New York and sell it out...if he announced he was playing a club in Raleigh, North Carolina, 20 people might show up. Having gone to school in Syracuse and worked in radio there, I was very familiar with the Benny mystique. So, it was actually kind of special that he was there.

The gig was pushed back multiple times the next night and we started very, very late. So late, in fact, that the House of Blues closed and very few people got to see the show. It was a real bummer and the last time I would perform with the band. As the years went on, I went to fewer and fewer conventions and the band dissolved anyway – but singing "Honkytonk Women" on stage at Tipitina's was the first time I realized that I truly was living my life vicariously through musicians. There is no greater rush than performing live.

CHAPTER 17

MY CHRIS FARLEY MOMENTS

If Ringo was my perfect meeting of a musician I was a big fan of, there were some imperfections as well. One of my favorite Saturday Night Live sketches was the one where Chris Farley meets some of his favorite artists, gets starstruck, and proceeds to act like a bumbling idiot. Upon meeting Paul McCartney, Farley says, "You know how you say...the love you take is equal to the love you make?" Paul replies in the affirmative, to which Chris asks, "Is that true?"

My real life Chris Farley moment occurred in Toronto at an album release party for Lenny Kravitz. It was a super cool (naturally) club that had a giant spinning fan on the wall (like the kind you would expect to see in a movie about a German military aircraft maker). Lenny walked in wearing a fur coat and oversized sunglasses and as usual, my wife and I bided our time before making our approach.

I've been a fan of Lenny since I first heard "Let Love Rule". A copy of the promo CD came into the station when I was interning at X100, and although it wasn't a big song for the station, it was a staff favorite. The beatle-esque nature of the songs, perfect combination of electric and acoustic tracks and the epic crescendo of the title track had me locked in. So, when a record rep invited me to the launch party of Lenny's appropriately titled fifth album "5", it was a no-brainer to make the trip from Buffalo.

The first thing I said to Lenny was "I love the new album", which is always a fine way to start. It always makes the artist smile, because let's face it – they like hearing that they are loved (as we all do). So even if you're just stroking the ego...even if you've never heard one note of the album, it's a good move to say you like the album. Chances are you won't get quizzed on it. Not long prior to the party, Lenny had filmed a Levi's commercial and I had decided this was a subject I would bring up.

See, leading up to the question, my wife and I had a pow-wow. It's like the Geneva Convention, trying to figure out what you're going to say to someone you're a fan of can be difficult because you don't want to say the wrong thing. You don't want to act like an idiot. The guy that the artist says later to his manager about, "Who the hell was that douchebag earlier tonight?" Yeah, you want to avoid that situation. In the moment, the Levi's commercial seemed like a perfect topic. A) It was current. B) It was about Lenny. C'mon , he'll love to talk about himself. Dale Carnegie stuff. C) He would likely have a story to tell about the filming. See B.

Ok, conversation starts simply enough, cordial, "Hey man, love the new album". "Thanks! I really appreciate that." Ok, smooth, lead in to the next question, here we go. "Hey Lenny, you know that new Levi's commercial you're in?" Lenny: "Yeah". Me: "That was cool".

I felt like a total douchebag, and even more so when Lenny abruptly stopped talking, said "thanks for coming", and slinked away.

I have been very fortunate in my career to have attended the Grammy Awards seven times. The first time I was selected to go was the only time of the seven that it was held in New York City at Madison Square Garden (the Grammys would later abandon the rotating NY-LA system for a permanent home at the Staples Center in Los Angeles.) The trip was, by and large, made by morning shows from various radio stations across America. When the opportunity came about in early

1997 for K101 to broadcast from the Grammy Awards, instead of sending our legendary morning host, our leader shouted in the meeting, "I think we should send J. Diamond!!" (J. Diamond was my first airname and the one I used at K101. This wasn't the only time he shouted this line at a meeting in such a way that would work in my favor. It also scored me a free trip to Mexico thanks to an Alaska Airlines promotion – more on that later).

So here's a guy who's worked on the airwaves in San Francisco for decades being passed over on a Grammy Awards trip, one of radio's greatest perks, for the Music Director and host of the Saturday Night disco show? Perhaps I had so much integrity and couth that I would defer to him and say, "There's no way I could take that trip. Morning shows from around the country will be there and it will look silly for me to be calling back to the station while others are broadcasting live. Besides, he has the tenure and reputation and has earned the right to go on this venture." Or perhaps I would keep my mouth shut.

Let's start with the fact that my accommodations were at the Marriott Marquis in Times Square, which didn't suck. Or, that the first day of the trip involved sitting around a large conference table at the headquarters of Arista Records as the one and only founder of Arista (and arguably the person with the greatest ears for a hit), Clive Davis played some new music for us at earsplitting decibel levels. As a Music Director in a major market, my trip to New York for the Grammys had sway and I was invited to this meeting. Only about 10 people were around the table, with Clive at the head of the table and Vice President of A&R Keith Naftaly (who was previously a legendary Program Director at KMEL/San Francisco) standing over one shoulder. Mr. Davis wore a suit as I imagined he would, and felt extremely intimidating. Clive would play the song, then go around the table – one by one –

and ask for our opinions on the track. It should have been a little nerve-wracking, but despite the fact that I was nearly breathless and worried about what I would say when it got to be my turn, I found it to be more awesome than anything. (The first song we listened to was an Ace of Base cover of Bananarama's "Cruel Summer" and I said it was a perfect release for summer and would do well. It stiffed.)

After this meeting, we went to Atlantic Records, where their artists and musicians were brought around for interviews, and I was faced with the aforementioned awkward position of having to act as the liaison between the artist and our legendary host back at the station. The first artist up was Jewel, who at this point had already scored massive hits at our Adult Contemporary format with a trio of singles - "Who Will Save Your Soul", "Foolish Games", and "You Were Meant For Me". Although these songs were very important to the format, everybody - and I mean everybody – knew just three things about Jewel. Number one – she's from Alaska (not many artists make it big from the arctic). Number two – she has a giant gap in her teeth. And number three, and the story that had been played out in probably hundreds if not thousands of interviews over the two years that preceded my visit with her, was that she lived in a van down by the river. Well, she lived in a van in San Diego when she got her break. Jewel was also somewhat notorious for being a little on the bitchy side so when I handed the phone to Jewel to talk to the show back at the studio, it was unfortunate that the conversation went like this. "So, you're from Alaska, huh?" Jewel (exasperated look on her face only I could see): "Yeah". Long pause. "What was it like living in a van?" I felt bad. I don't think Jewel answered any more questions after that. I don't think he wanted to ask any more questions. Jewel should have just taken it like a champ (she was talking to the morning show on a top rated station in the #4 market in America), but I also felt her pain from hearing the same two questions she'd probably been asked in every interview between 1995 and 1997. I felt for our amazing jock who should have been in New York but instead was stuck inside a control room while his music director was at the headquarters of Atlantic Records meeting celebrities.

During the Grammy Awards, we were positioned in the "press room" which, in the antiquated Madison Square Garden, looked like a dungeon. It had no windows, no air conditioning, and no view of the awards. Basically, you had a spot at a long table and your own landline phone to use – but you had to have your own calling card. That's right kids, I didn't have a cell phone yet in 1997. There were a couple of monitors on which you could watch the awards show going on in the arena, but that was your only feed to the action. There was a big blue backdrop that was splashed with the Grammy logo, so that winning artists would shuffle into the room, hold their Grammys in their hands, and photographers would get the money shot. This space is where artists like Adele and Eric Clapton, in the years in which they won an inordinate number of awards, were captured on film right afterwards.

Interviews would take place in this room, but most artists would only do one or two interviews if you were lucky. Considering the artists came into this room every time they won an award, they usually wanted to go right back to their seats. Plus, there was no way someone like me would land an interview when I was competing with outlets like New York radio stations and "Entertainment Tonight".

I'll never forget when Stevie Wonder sat right across to speak with the radio station next to me. I at least got a chance to say hi to one of my favorite performers, albeit for a few seconds. But the real excitement for me came when Dave Matthews Band won a Grammy for their album, "Under the Table and Dreaming". At 25, I was very much in the DMB demo at the time and in the few years after this I would road trip to every show within about 6 hours driving distance (taking in over thirty shows in all). When an artist wins a Grammy, they wait in a holding area of sorts right outside the press room until they are called in. As soon as I saw on the monitor that they had won, I sneaked towards the door and waited for their arrival. I figured I would have two, maybe three minutes in the hallway to meet my favorite band.

The plan worked like a charm. Up the hallway walked all the members of the band, stopping in front of the door while the attendant instructed them to wait their turn for photos and interviews. Seeing that the band's namesake was indisposed, I jumped right over to violinist Boyd Tinsley and told him how much I enjoyed seeing him play. I marveled at how he would play "Ants Marching" with reckless abandon, breaking string after string without a care in the world. My conversation with Boyd was going very well, and he was gracious and appreciative of my support.

That's when I saw Dave was alone and swooped over without even saying goodbye or thank you to Boyd. I knew I probably only had a few seconds before they would be called into the room.

"Dave", I started. "I just want to tell you that you seem like you'd be a really cool guy to hang out with."

WHAT??

He chuckled, said "thanks" and was whisked into the press room, where he surely wondered where the hell that stalker came from.

What a douchebag....

CHAPTER 18

YES, IT REALLY WAS A PURPLE THRONE

On April 20, 1997, I got to see Prince for the first time. "Purple Rain" was a transformative album for me in middle school, and I was highly jacked up for this show. The concert was at the San Jose State Events Center, featured the Purple One bounding about the stage playing every instrument (including the intense humping of the piano), and – surprise – showcased the Bay Area's own Carlos Santana in the encore on four songs, including his own "Soul Sacrifice".

Prince was known for legendary after-parties following his live gigs, and this one would be at the DNA Lounge in San Francisco. Since the show ended around 11p and it takes 45 minutes to drive from San Jose up to The City, this would be a very long night. Plus, you know Prince wasn't going to be the first one to arrive. So around 1am, a large entourage walked in comprised of 6 tall muscular men surrounding Prince, who was so tiny he couldn't even be seen in the middle of the mass. About 15 minutes later, I was escorted by the label rep into the VIP area where there was but one guest, Prince (and his manager) and he was sitting on a purple throne.

I was totally starstruck.

When you're taught how to ask great questions in an interview, rule number one is never ask "yes" or "no" questions. I should have heeded this rule when I met Prince. Come to think of it, I wish I had even asked a question! After the label guy introduced me, and Prince stared in my direction, all I could do was shower praise on the guy. Tell him how much his music meant to me. What an underrated guitarist I thought he was. Many artists would have taken that as a cue to steer the conversation, or at least, you know, say "thank you". But Prince didn't say thanks. In fact, he didn't say a word. After 90 seconds of babbling about the joy his music brought to me and feeding his ego, the Purple One just stared at me. It was so awkward that his manager chimed in to make me feel better, all while Prince continued to stare.

It wouldn't be long before I was walking back downstairs, a little dumbfounded about the one-sided conversation. Prince did not say one solitary word to me. But I don't hold any grudge towards Prince because – admit it – even though his behavior was bizarre, does it really surprise you?

Didn't think so.

My favorite Prince story is the one Questlove of The Roots tells about the time he's asked by Prince's team to bring some friends to a roller skating party. Most people with Questlove aren't interested (!) but Eddie Murphy comes along. After being made to wait for hours, Prince shows up, takes Questlove's cell phone away (no pictures!), opens a giant briefcase in the middle of the rink, pulls out a glowing pair of skates, and proceeds to skate as well as he sings.

That seems just about as Prince as you can get.

I was returning from lunch, listening to Colin Cowherd's sports radio show when I found out Prince died. It was the first time I can recall uncontrollably weeping upon hearing of a celebrity's passing.

CHAPTER 19

WHOA, MEXICO – SEACREST, OUT!

The year between summer 1996 and summer 1997 was an exhilarating one for me. In June, 1996 I was on the beach on the Jersey Shore with my finance and brother-in-law when a call came in from the Program Director of K101 in San Francisco. He was offering me a job as Music Director, it paid $32,000 a year, and the company would pay to move me. He took a real chance on me. It was a shock to the system of our world – we were getting married in Rochester, New York in two months. Jennifer had barely even been to the West Coast, maybe one or two visits. So in the middle of trying to plan a wedding, we would be moving everything three thousand miles across country to work for a company I'd never worked at and for a man I had never even met in person.

My dream job was to program KFOG in San Francisco, a deliciously eclectic station with jocks as quirky as the music that I'd grown up listening to. Phil Zachary, one of my bosses in Raleigh later in my career, liked to say that he used to think the measure of a great Program Director was whether or not he could create that "major market sound". It wasn't until later in his career that he realized that the greatest PDs were judged on how well they reflected their market. By that criteria, KFOG was the all-time kingpin – a radio station that so encompassed the culture and vibe of the Bay Area, it could not possibly be successful anywhere else.

K101, however, was a pretty great offering in its own right. When I say I grew up listening to KFOG, the truth was that I grew up listening to every radio station in San Francisco. I didn't really know it at the time, but I was a radio geek of the highest order. A kid who called DJs at music stations to make requests, called sports stations to weigh in on topics, and recorded himself on his Panasonic tape recorder with the little orange button pretending to be M Dung, Don Bleu, Dr. Don Rose, Rick Chase, or any of the legendary SF DJs of the day. K101 was a heritage station – familiar call letters with a reliable brand. The opportunity to work there was too tempting to resist. The one and only Rick Shaw ("Rick Shaw, ladies and gentlemen") held down afternoons – that was until the PD brought in a rising star from Los Angeles named Ryan Seacrest.

The boss was let go around 6 months into my tenure at K101 and I was made Interim Program Director at age 24. When I tell people I worked with Ryan Seacrest, the questions are always the same. "Is he gay?" (just stop). "Is he a primadonna?" (not really). If you question Ryan's talent or think he was lucky, I vigorously defend him. I've not seen anyone in the business work as hard as Seacrest. While at K101, he was still flying back and forth from San Francisco to Los Angeles to film specials for networks like E! and the Discovery Channel. He hosted a game show called "Click" for Merv Griffin. You want to talk about someone who had goals and achieved them? He wanted to be like Rick Dees – so he took Rick's job as morning host at KIIS-FM in Los Angeles. He wanted to be like Casey Kasem – so he succeeded Casey as host of American Top 40. He wanted to be like Dick Clark – so he co-hosted New Year's Rockin' Eve with the legend himself until ultimately taking the show over as Dick's health declined and his inevitable passing. Some would be perfectly happy as host of "American Idol", a gig that on its own I'm sure paid him plenty. But Ryan loves radio so much he still hosts his morning show in LA each day and records syndicated content for iHeart Radio stations across the country. Then there's his production company and the many other projects he's involved in. I was fortunate to work with him and enjoyed our lunches and cocktail hours. We once had lunch together at a small café just down the street from K101 and just swapped radio stories like the radio geeks we were. Another time a bunch of us went out after work to a bar/restaurant near the Embarcadero and were having a great time over drinks when a group of four guys showed up and Ryan introduced us. They were the four umpires working the A's series in Oakland that week and this was their off day. Ryan knew the crew and had invited them to the gathering. Because of how engaging he is and a tremendous work ethic, the guy has always been connected...to everyone. I'm a fan.

Now imagine you're in a conference room and your role at K101 is Music Director. The only show you host is a Saturday night disco show (oh, it was the biggest Saturday night show in town – the gays loved me!). Sitting next to you is one of the most recognizable morning hosts in San Francisco radio history. The sales manager is telling the room about a client, Alaska Airlines, which is starting new service to Ixtapa-Zihuatenejo, Mexico. Alaska would like to send a K101 DJ to Ixtapa to experience the vacation and report back on it. By all means the morning host should have been the one to take this trip and I'm sure assumed he would do so until the General Manager shouted out, "You know who should take this trip?" The room waits with baited breath. "J. Diamond!!!" (silence). He'd done it again. He wanted to send a kid who hosted one show a week on an incredible vacation to Mexico?? Maybe he felt bad he was only paying me $32,000 a year in one of the world's most expensive cities.

So, my new wife Jennifer and I went on Alaska Airlines to Ixtapa/Zihuantanejo. First, some context because most don't instantly recognize the name of the city. You know the place where Andy Dufrain tells Red to meet him at the end of

"Shawshank Redemption"? On the beach with the bluest ocean you've ever seen? That's Zihuatanejo. It is a tiny fishing village, next to the slightly more modern Ixtapa and it is a spectacular area of Mexico. Not overpopulated with tourists like Cancun and Acapulco, Ixtapa is towards the end of Mexico in the central time zone and is breathtaking. We learned early on, however, that it would be an adventure when our connecting plane in Los Angeles ran over a tug which got stuck in the wheel. I had the window seat, but I wasn't paying attention to what was going on outside the window (naturally, I was focusing all my attention on my beautiful fiancee). There was a loud thump, a sound you never really want to hear on a plane but you think, "At least we're on the runway and...we're still here, so that's good". When I did look outside the window, there was the wing, and there was the tug, jammed right in the wheel. Since the wheel was bent to hell, we had to deplane from the tarmac and catch a shuttle back to the terminal and switch planes, so that delayed us for a couple hours. We would just have to have a couple of pre-game margaritas in the airport bar.

When we arrived in Itxapa, we were truly taken by its beauty and the hotel, the Westin Brisas Ixtapa, was unreal. It's carved into a mountain at an angle, and every room has its own private balcony that overlooks the hotel's private beach. We found that American money was going very far in Mexico, as even expensive hotel prices weren't all that unreasonable and we had more than one pitcher of sangria. That first night the airline hosted a welcome party for us at the hotel on the private beach, where the beer being sold was Sol – a brand I'd never seen in the U.S. to that point (now pretty much every store has it). We were told Corona was for tourists – the locals drink Sol, they said. When we went back to the hotel bar for a nightcap, the bar area was pretty rowdy, and there was one guy in particular who was really causing a scene. He was gyrating, palms on his head, the abs of his exposed stomach flying back and forth. This guy looked familiar – really familiar, but we couldn't place it. Then his pants came down. Full moon in the Brisas hotel bar. Turns out there was a reason he looked familiar but we couldn't place it – he was the younger brother of a very famous celebrity and they look a lot alike. It was Frank Stallone, brother of Sylvester. He was filming a movie in Ixtapa. He may have been best known at the time as the subject of a recurring bit on Saturday Night Live, in which Norm McDonald would blame all actual news events on him. This was right around the time we were mooned in Mexico.

The trip was truly amazing. I was introduced for the first time to tequila that doesn't cause tequila face (Don Julio), spoke Spanish to our driver during a scavenger hunt (which gave us a unique advantage), did shots on our back at Carlos and Charlie's, went paragliding, and had the time of our lives. Who knew the return home would be the most exciting thing of all? The Ixtapa airport is small – it was redone two years later, but the airport was essentially one building with a handful of gates. Jennifer and I had just placed our carry-on luggage on the x-ray conveyor belt when we heard a rumbling sound that progressively increased in volume. We could easily spot the palm trees blowing rapidly outside the gates. We had already made it past security when the rumble grew louder, as we watched a large Mexicana Airlines jet turn towards the gates. We thought it odd that the pilot was turning the plane so close to the terminal, but figured protocol might be different at a small airport. We were standing next to a group of people that included a uniformed pilot, who out of the blue said (in Spanish), "Come with me into the bathroom" just as the sound of the engines grew deafening. Our small group followed the pilot into the bano when we could hear the sound of glass breaking. Lots of glass. There was screaming and running and mayhem – we peeked outside the bathroom to see shards of glass flying everywhere. The engine sound got so loud it could have rivaled a Bon Jovi concert circa 1987 – and then it faded into the distance. When we emerged from the bathroom, many of the windows that looked out onto the tarmac had shattered. Glass was strewn everywhere, and many of the patrons had cuts all over their faces and arms. It looked like a horror movie, and fortunately it appeared nobody had been seriously injured. The pilot had revved the engine too hot, too close to the terminal. We thought it interesting that the pilot shuffled us into the bathroom before the incident actually occurred. How did he know? The pilot turned to us and said, "That guy is a terrible pilot".

CHAPTER 20

MARRY BIG OR DON'T MARRY AT ALL

On the morning of 7 days before my wedding day, I woke up with the most excruciating pain I had ever felt to that point or have felt since. I was literally screaming out loud while holding my right palm to my right cheek. "What? What is it? What's going on?", Jennifer wanted to know. "My mouth! My mouth!", I was howling. Because it was a Sunday, I could not get in to see a dentist until the next day so until then I would have to get through on a heavy dose of ice and ibuprofen. Although it didn't occur to me at first, I knew soon after the pain began what was going on...and it was my own damn fault. The family dentist had been telling me since the age of 14 that I needed to have my wisdom teeth pulled out. "Because one day", she warned, "the teeth will impact and it will be very painful and there's no need to let it get to that point." "Do I have time?", I would always ask. "Yes", was always the reply. "How much?", was my follow up. That answer was always the same. "I don't know". I finally had my answer. August 3, 1997.

When I did get in to see Jennifer's family dentist the next day, he lightly touched one of the wisdom teeth. "Does this hurt?" "Oh!!!! Ahhhhh!!!" Ummm...yeah. Now it was official. I had to have all four teeth pulled out but now we were only four days until the rehearsal dinner, five days until a golf outing with invited guests, and six days until the wedding. "You have two choices", I was told by the dentist. "You can get the procedure done this week. I've checked with the surgeon and he can get you in this Wednesday. But there is a significant chance there will be swelling." Thinking about how I would look in the pictures, I could feel Jennifer's stare searing through me like a grill to steak. "Or?", I inquired. "Or we can give you good drugs and you can get it done when you come back." I selected the latter.

The drugs worked wonderfully and the wedding was spectacular. So much fun, in fact, that my grandfather kept paying the band additional $100 bills to keep playing that Sunday night. So much fun that the party continued in my mother's suite until 1:30 in the morning. So much fun, in fact, that after Jennifer and I returned to our suite we fell asleep and missed our flight. This was an exceptionally bad situation, since we were taking a cruise and had to get to Miami or we would literally miss the boat. "I'm sorry", the airline agent told us at the airport. "There's no way." And at that, Jennifer began crying. A really good cry, too. Heavy, scattered breathing, full on tears streaming down her face. "B-b-but it's our honeymooooon!", she wailed. "I don't believe this. I cannot believe this." The male agent quietly said "Let me see what I can do", and started clicking away at the keyboard. The only option was to fly through two different cities to get to Miami from Rochester. What's worse was that we would need to fly standby on both flights. There was a real possibility the adventure could end in the Baltimore or Tampa airports.

With very little time to spare, we did make it to the ship (although my luggage did not for the first couple of days). Because I was having a decent amount of cocktails on the ship and I'd been on heavy sedatives for a week, I slept more on our honeymoon than anything else. When we returned I got those wisdom teeth pulled out. Maybe I should have listened to the family dentist.

CHAPTER 21

I DIDN'T REALIZE I WAS TALKING TO JACK BAUER

Singer/Songwriter Jude Cole was one of my favorite artists in the 90's and one evening in San Francisco my friend Steve and I went to Slim's to see Jude play. Slim's is a well-known club in the South of Market district that was opened in 1988 by Boz Scaggs. Surrounded by brick and a New Orleans themed bar with chandeliers hanging from the ceiling, Slim's is the kind of place anyone could show up on any night. In between the opening act and Jude's set, Steve excused himself to go to the bathroom and I started a conversation with a guy who was standing by himself, sporting some facial hair and wearing a baseball cap.

It was an engaging conversation – the guy was delighted that I was such a fan of Jude's, and we spoke at length about his catalog of music. The dialogue veered into ancillary subjects like the weather, the San Francisco Giants, and great restaurants around town. The conversation was so enjoyable, in fact, that it continued for about 20 minutes - well after Steve had returned from relieving himself, but Steve didn't come over to interrupt or join in.

When I had completed the conversation with the stranger, I walked back over to Steve when he promptly asked, "Who were you talking to?" "I don't know", I responded. "Why?" "That guy was a dead ringer for Kiefer Sutherland", Steve remarks. "You think so?" I turned to get a second look but he was gone. Didn't think too much about it until, towards the end of the headlining set, Jude says, "I'd like to bring up my best friend to do a song with me...Mr. Kiefer Sutherland."

CHAPTER 22

DUDE, WHERE'S MY TRUCK?

They would say that, when your CBS Radio station was on the outs, the president of the company – Mel Karmazin – would beckon the General Manager to the pool at that year's manager's conference for a "poolside chat". A poolside chat with Mel was the last thing you wanted as a GM and in 1999, word got around that Jeff Silver had a poolside chat with Mel.

You can tell when things are going south – higher ups start acting differently around you, making less eye contact. There seem to be more closed doors around the office. The most obvious sign of a doomed radio station is the veritable closing of the checkbook. The company just stops spending money on things. Anything. Everything. That research project you do every spring, the direct mail campaign, even the koozies and keychains for remotes. Gone, gone, gone....gotta stay "lean", you know. Plus, there are people with ties walking around everywhere. "The suits".

I hated how I found out the format was changing. I was brought into Jeff's office and told that the station would be changed from Pop Alternative to a Jammin' Oldies station which focused on rhythmic R&B. "When?", I wanted to know. "In 45 minutes", he replied. They wanted to see how I was going to react. I mean, sure, Alice @ 92.9 was my baby and certainly I was going to be disappointed, but to blindside me like that? I'm a professional. "It's business", as Don Corleone so eloquently put it. I could have helped with the transition. On the other hand, maybe it was better that they didn't tell me so I didn't have to deal with that stress for months. But I still would have preferred to have been told. Because it was me (along with Jeff) that had to walk up to the studio, pop "It's

The End of the World As We Know It" on the air, ask our midday jock Sarah to step aside, and start some R&B track to launch the new station while Sarah wailed in the corner.

You always remember the first and last song of a format but I don't remember the first song of that station because I honestly didn't care. CBS was changing Pop Alternative (also referred to as Modern Adult Contemporary) stations to Jammin' Oldies all over the country and I felt it was the flavor of the month and wouldn't last long (I turned out to be right). That's why, when Jeff asked me to program the Jammin' Oldies station I said no because "I'm not going to fail twice in this building". Jeff respected my stance but because I was under contract for another year, he wasn't going to let me sit on the sidelines. So, when the PD of the country station got a dream gig at another country station in Chicago, I became Assistant Program Director and Afternoon Drive for WYRK while I looked for a new gig.

Country radio is fun. The listeners are extremely passionate, loyal, knowledgeable, and friendly. The artists are accessible and go out of their way for the fans (a lesson rock stars would do well to learn). My 8 months in country radio were some of the greatest 8 months of my life. As Assistant Program Director, I was suddenly just "one of the guys" now, and I was joining the staff at happy hours and outings I was never invited to as a PD. Plus, I developed a stronger relationship with Jeff during this time. Without the pressures of getting called to his office 15 times a day, we spent lots of quality time out of the office on lunches or the wife and I getting invited to his home for dinner. He was a terrific advisor as well, genuinely helping me look for my next opportunity.

First came a call to program 98 PXY in Rochester, a station my wife grew up listening to as she's from Webster, a suburb of the Flower City. That interview went well – the General Manager asked me to sit in a room and do a "monitor" of the station (which is programming speak for "listening and taking notes"). The GM wants to see what the programmer picks up – what the station is doing well, not so well, and could be doing better. When it was all said and done, I was second to the guy that got the job, Norm on the Barstool. Generally I would be ticked that I lost out on a gig to a guy named Norm on the Barstool, but he had been the assistant under the previous PD, so really it was his to lose and I'm sure he was quite talented.

Next came the PD opening at one of America's most successful Hot Adult Contemporary stations, Mix 94.7 in one of America's most awesomest cities, Austin, Texas. Hot A/C was my background. I started my career at Y94, a very successful station in the format in Syracuse; interim programmed one of the legendary A/C stations in America (and one I grew up listening to), K101; and programmed Alice in Buffalo, a Pop Alternative version of the format. That was actually a pretty good fit, considering Austin is an alternative kind of town.

Mix was a CBS station, which was helpful since I was already in the company. My GM knew the GM in Austin and I remember when he got off the phone with that GM and told me, "I really warmed this one up for you." Then, while sitting in a conference room at CBS/Buffalo, I did a phone interview with the Austin GM that went so well, he told me, "I know I shouldn't be so presumptuous, Jay, but I really want to hire you. I think meeting you in person will be simply a formality. I really look forward to meeting you." The interest level on his part was so high, he had his assistant book a flight for me within the next couple of days.

I wanted the Austin gig very badly. I had visited Austin

once before and loved it. It was hip, fun, young, and reminded me quite a bit of my hometown, San Francisco. After having spent the majority of the past seven years in the frozen tundra of upstate New York in cities that were in deep population decline, it would be exciting to move to a growing city. Plus, one of the things that made Buffalo such a challenge was that it was a start-up. New formats are so difficult because listeners are so habitual. As a Program Director, taking the reins of an established station isn't always as exciting, but it's a far less risky play. I had a morning show disaster in Buffalo, and I thought working with JB and Sandy, their very popular show in Austin, could also be a terrific move for my career.

The station set me up with a rental car, and I was highly amused when I arrived at the airport that it was in fact a rental truck (welcome to Texas!). I drove the Ford F-150 to a restaurant near the station for lunch, as I had about an hour to kill before my appointment with the GM. Following lunch, I made the short drive to the station, which was part of a very large office building with a sprawling parking lot that featured outdoor parking and an indoor deck. I parked the truck, walked into the building, took the elevator up to their floor, and announced my arrival with the receptionist.

The fact was, I was incredibly relaxed. I already had a home run phone interview in the bag, this was a format I was totally comfortable with, and it was a beautiful sunny day in Austin. "Jay", the receptionist beckoned. "Follow me, he will see you now." She led me down the hall to a large dark wood laden office where a large man walked towards me, and then stopped as if surprised. He looked me up and down as if we were at the OK Corral, sat down at his desk, and firmly asked me, "Well, you look like you're 12 years old. How does your staff deal with that?"

Maybe I shouldn't have been, but I was stunned. Frozen.

Never mind the fact that it's inappropriate (and borderline illegal) to ask someone about their age in a job interview. I felt every bit of positivity and confidence I had walking into that building pour out of me like water from a fountain. I honestly didn't know how to answer that question. The truth was that my employees always respected me because I treated them fairly and with respect. That I brought a positive attitude to the workplace. Most importantly, regardless of my age, I was always good at my job and led by example. And you know, that's what's I should have said. But when you're thrown off your game by a very intimidating person, the response was more like, "I...I don't think it matters."

I found out later why this was a big deal to him. The PD before me was young and clearly had some respect issues with the staff, a hiring mistake the GM was determined not to repeat. And that day, sitting in his office, I was still only all of 26 years old. Needless to say, the rest of the interview didn't matter, although it probably didn't go as bad as it did in my head. After spending the night at my hotel that evening, I discovered JB and Sandy were doing a live broadcast the next morning and since I had a rental truck, I decided to throw a Hail Mary pass. I drove to the remote to meet them.

It went perfectly fine. I introduced myself, complimented them on their work (they were a very good morning show), and bought one of the t-shirts they were selling for charity which I know probably made me look like a total kiss ass but I knew I was in the hole on this interview and I figured if I could pull an end around with the morning show, maybe I had an outside shot. Morning shows (especially highly rated ones) often have more pull than anyone at a radio station so it was worth a shot.

I had lunch with the GM that day and had a more formal sit down with JB and Sandy and then it was time to say goodbye. I felt better about the second day and thought, although age was probably going to cost me the job, I'd done my best to rebound and keep myself in the running. I walked out to the parking lot and was certain – I mean 100% certain without a shadow of a doubt – where I had parked that truck and it was not there. There was an empty space in the spot where I was 100% certain I had parked that truck. I walked up and down and all around that lot and did not see the truck. My heart was racing and I didn't know what to do, but I was sure I parked that truck there.

I took the elevator back up to the station and told the receptionist, "Someone stole my rental truck." "Oh my", she said. "Are you sure?" "I'm positive.", I told her. The GM overheard the conversation and now he's in the mix. "Do you want me to call the police?", she asked. Knowing with 100% certainty that I had parked the truck in the spot that no longer had a truck parked in it, I said "Yes, call the police. I'll go wait for them out in the lot." Well. While waiting for the police to arrive, I walked to some places in the lot I had not roamed during my first browse around, and there in front of me, in shiny red, was the truck. I hung my head. I did not know whether or not to laugh or cry. And....there was the police car, followed by the receptionist and the General Manager to follow up on what was going on.

I looked at the police officer and the GM, and softly said, "Umm...I found the truck."

You're shocked to learn I didn't get the Austin gig, aren't you?

Early photographic evidence that I was destined to attend
Syracuse University, where the number 44 is revered.

The Z89 softball team. The Syracuse University radio station
is the greatest media classroom on Earth.

WJPZ • SYRACUSE

PROGRAM DIRECTOR: JEREMY NACHLIS   WEEK OF: MAY 25, 1992
MUSIC DIRECTOR: JON MARSH

TW	LW			
H 1	1	JUMP	Kris Kross	RUFFHOUSE
H 2	2	MY LOVIN'	En Vogue	EAST WEST
H 3	4	IN THE CLOSET	Michael Jackson	EPIC
H 4	8	IF YOU ASKED ME TO	Celine Dion	EPIC
5	7	I WILL REMEMBER YOU	Amy Grant	A&M
6	3	LIVE AND LEARN	Joe Public	COLUMBIA
7	5	WILL YOU MARRY ME?	Paula Abdul	VIRGIN
H 8	12	JUST ANOTHER DAY	Jon Secada	SBK
9	14	YOU WON'T SEE ME CRY	Wilson Phillips	SBK
10	13	DAMN, I WISH I WAS YOUR...	Sophie B. Hawkins	COLUMBIA
11	15	DO IT TO ME	Lionel Richie	MOTOWN
12	6	AIN'T 2 PROUD 2 BEG	T.L.C.	LA FACE
13	18	UNDER THE BRIDGE	Red Hot Chili Peppers	WB
14	20	I'LL BE THERE	Mariah Carey	COLUMBIA
15	17	LIFT ME UP	Howard Jones	ELEKTRA
16	21	THE BEST THINGS IN LIFE...	L. Vandross/J. Jackson	A&M
17	9	MONEY DON'T MATTER 2 NIGHT	Prince & The N.P.G.	PAISLEY PK
18	22	SLOW MOTION	Color Me Badd	GIANT
19	25	TENNESSEE	Arrested Development	CHRYSALIS
20	24	JUST FOR TONIGHT	Vanessa Williams	WING
21	10	I'M THE ONE YOU NEED	Jody Watley	MCA
22	27	SILENT PRAYER	Shanice	MOTOWN
23	26	STEEL BARS	Michael Bolton	COLUMBIA
24	11	TAKE TIME	Chris Walker	ELEKTRA
25	30	BABY GOT BACK	Sir Mix-A-Lot	DEF AMER.
26	29	T.L.C.	Linear	ATLANTIC
27	16	MAKE IT HAPPEN	Mariah Carey	COLUMBIA
28	34	WARM IT UP	Kris Kross	RUFFHOUSE
29	D	WISHING ON A STAR	Cover Girls	EPIC
30	D	KEEP ON WALKIN'	Ce Ce Peniston	A&M
31	D	NEVER SATISFIED	Good 2 Go	GIANT
32	D	BABY BABY BABY	T.L.C.	LA FACE
33	A	WHATEVER IT TAKES	Troop	ATLANTIC
34	A	GIVING HIM SOMETHING...	En Vogue	EAST WEST
35	A	TAKE THIS HEART	Richard Marx	CAPITOL

ADDS
#33, #34, #35

My first Program Director position was at Z89 and I don't
mind telling you, for all y'all suckers that don't know, this
playlist is not wiggity-wiggity-wiggity wack.

So kids, they had these things called cassettes and disc jockeys used to record their shows on them so Program Directors could critique them in an "aircheck" to tell them how much they sucked.

Me in the Y94 studio. Nice monitor! State of the art!

Barenaked Ladies bassist Jim Creeggan (2nd from left)
and I met when I was promoting a concert with his side
project, The Brothers Creeggan, in Buffalo. The band never
made it over the border from Canada (twice). That's my wife
Jennifer between me and singer Ed Robertson.

PRESENTED TO
JAY NACHLIS
TO COMMEMORATE RIAA CERTIFIED
SALES OF MORE THAN
4,000,000 COPIES OF THE
REPRISE RECORDS
COMPACT DISC AND CASSETTE
AND 100,000 COPIES OF THE
WARNER REPRISE MUSIC VIDEO
"THE DANCE"

Record labels used to give out lots of plaques like this
often when they had money to spend in the old days.

One year before shaving my head for St. Baldrick's, I grew it out for about 6 months then got it blown out. "I'd like the Phil Spector, please".

St. Baldrick's after photo. Over 13 years as a host and shavee, I'm proud to say I've personally raised over $20,000 for childhood cancer research.

Lenny Kravitz is one of my all-time favorites. One of the two guys in this picture is cool.

Contrary to popular belief, some chicks dig Rush (like my wife). Rush concerts are the only ones at which the men's restroom lines are longer.

Me, Harry Potter-era.

I always regretted that my mom let me quit guitar
lessons. It's never too late – in my late 30's, I took lessons
and performed during NHL All-Star Weekend in downtown
Raleigh with the 96rock band, Radiowave.

The 96rock staff with Stormy and the "Cane Vic" – before
it was destroyed by Hurricanes fans after their 2006 Stanley
Cup win.

When you broadcast live from the Grammys, you're backstage on the Thursday and Friday afternoon before the awards show. You get a few minutes with a celebrity, then they are rushed off and another one sits down. It is an unbelievable adrenaline rush.

My favorite publicity shot. During the "Foster and Blade" years on 96rock, we broadcasted live from Raleigh's Hibernian Pub Friday afternoons in the summer. The legs and heels belong to promo queen Cody Butler.

I was up for a Billboard award for Music Director of the Year.
My mother recognized the Prince of Darkness and I did not.
Dork.

I wasn't just living the dream in radio – I got to fulfill
dreams because of it. This is me right before my first flight
lesson at Blue Line Aviation.

After I introduced Robin Williams during what would be his final concert tour, he thanked me and said what a great job I had done. This meant the world to me.

Moments after I told Ringo how much The Beatles meant
to me, he called over the photographer for this shot.

CHAPTER 23

(REALLY) MAKING UP FOR MISSING ONE OF MY FAVORITE BANDS IN HIGH SCHOOL

Just after 10 a.m. on November 11th, 1987, I was a sophomore at McAteer High School in San Francisco making my way through the halls to the next class when word got out. U2 was going to play a free concert in Justin Hermann Plaza in the Embarcadero at Noon. That day. As in, two hours from then. Mind you, this was before cell phones and before the internet – so it was old school viral marketing at its finest. The DJ at 106 KMEL had gone on the air just moments earlier to make the announcement. U2 was touring behind "The Joshua Tree" and by this point of the tour had already released the three juggernaut singles from the album. "With Or Without You", "I Still Haven't Found What I'm Looking For", and "Where The Streets Have No Name" were on the radio all day, every day, and the lads from Ireland were arguably the biggest band on the planet.

Later in the week, U2 was scheduled to play back-to-back shows in Oakland at the Coliseum. They had played Denver three nights earlier, and had a show scheduled in Vancouver the next night – so from an itinerary standpoint, coming from Denver to San Francisco to go up to Vancouver and then back down to Oakland was unusual – but then again, the thought of U2 playing a free show was highly unusual.

This is the part of the story where I should be telling you that I did the right thing. That, knowing that school will go on tomorrow and there will only be one shot to see a free U2 show, I immediately hopped on a bus and sped directly to the

93

Embarcadero where I saw the band perform a charged version of "All Along The Watchtower". That I saw the controversial moment when, during the performance of "Pride (In The Name of Love)", Bono hopped up on the Valliancourt Fountain and spray painted the words "Rock and Roll Stops the Traffic". Bono would later have to apologize for defacing the sculpture, but paid for the repair and invited the artist on stage during the Oakland shows later that week. I'd love to tell you that I saw all of that, but I didn't.

I was a good boy and stayed in school.

But hey, it's not like there's any reminders around that I blew it that day....well, except for the fact that the performance is immortalized in U2's concert film, "Rattle and Hum".

The good news? Although it would be another year before I'd start interning at X100 and I had no idea at the time that I would become a radio Program Director with access to unthinkable perks, karma made sure the favor was returned. It only took 10 years.

June 19, 1997 was the first time I saw U2 in concert and it was, to say the least, an extreme disappointment. We had excellent seats for the second night of a two-night stand at the Oakland Coliseum Stadium, and Oasis opened the bill. Unfortunately that evening, Bono's voice was in terrible shape. The entire show lasted around 90 minutes, Edge constantly tried to pick up Bono on the vocal parts in which he was weak, and the show left me even more despondent that I missed my opportunity to see the band a decade earlier at their peak.

A month later, I would accept my first full-fledged Program Director position at Alice @ 92.9 in Buffalo, New York. Buffalo is only a 90 minute drive from Toronto and that was where U2 would begin Leg 3 of their North American tour, at Skydome. U2 played Tel Aviv on September 30th, and then they took a month off before the Toronto show. Certainly a product of being in the right place at the right time, my wife and I were invited to Toronto for the U2 show. We had an awesome room at the Intercontinental Hotel right on Front Street and seconds away from the CN Tower. After a tremendous dinner, we made our way to the venue and escorted to our seats...at the soundboard.

Watching this show was a completely different experience – not just because we were in the center of the stadium, but because the band was well rested. Bono sounded pristine, the band was tight and in good spirits, and after the show we were whisked through the annals of Skydome to a room with a full bar, snacks, and a pool table. I've been fortunate to have been to a bunch of meet and greets in my life, but this was the only one that featured billiards and nobody knew what to do with that. The first thought that runs through your mind is, "What if that's the *band's* pool table? Will we get in trouble if we play? What about the drinks? Maybe that's *their* bar?" See, there was no host per se, and there was no bartender. So at first, instead of partaking in the libations, everyone stood around twiddling their thumbs waiting for U2 to come out while a perfectly good pool table and untapped liquor sat there taunting us.

After about 25 minutes, it was my wife who cracked open the vodka, reached down for the billiards triangle, shouted out "Rack em up!", and the party began. That's all it needed. Soon everyone was having a drink, shooting pool, getting loose again (not like we didn't have a few cocktails during the show), and getting ready for U2. It's a good thing she did break the ice, because we ended up waiting nearly an hour for the band. But they didn't come to us.

The next thing we knew, band management was escorting

us through the dark, winding halls of SkyDome until we found ourselves in a red room filled with wardrobes on which outfit after outfit, costume after costume, hung. Perhaps it should have seemed obvious, but if you told us we were standing in U2's dressing room, I'm not sure I'd have believed you. One more door swung open past the wardrobe room, and standing there to greet the incoming group of the luckiest people on Earth was U2 bassist Adam Clayton. "C'mon in!", Clayton summoned, and as we did we looked around in disbelief. Standing on the left was one of the greatest guitarists of all-time, The Edge. Seated on a couch to our right was Bono. Adam made his way to the back of the room, and although I'm told he was there, drummer Larry Mullen, Jr. wove into the fabric of the crowd and we never actually saw him (he's the shy one in the band).

This meet and greet was extraordinary in so many different ways. For starters, of course, we were in the band's dressing room (not the first time for that, though – I was in Lenny Kravitz's dressing room in Philadelphia). The way the band was arranged was also highly unique. Generally bands are arranged in a lineup, so the pass holders can swiftly and efficiently make their way down the line for a handshake, and usually a picture and autograph though bands have varying rules on whether or not you get a picture or something signed. Here were the members of U2 spread around the room, so that each fan could spend some time with each one. Another slice of awesomeness was Adam Clayton handing out drinks. "You look thirsty", he remarked, opening the fridge and handing us a Heineken.

While most of the crowd flocked to Bono, we decided to make The Edge our first stop. Our conversation with him covered everything from guitar technique to what his favorite bands were at the time (he mentioned a very obscure techno band) to the instability in Sarajevo to my wife remarking how well he played on "Mysterious Ways" that night. We probably spent upwards of 20 minutes with The Edge, every moment feeling like we had known him for years. Clayton was our next stop on the backstage tour, during which he dropped a lesson in Irish etiquette when someone tried to prematurely interrupt our conversation – "Excuse me, but I'm in the middle of a conversation with these nice people. I'm going to need you to wait."

Finally it was on to Bono and because we were the last to see him, we could spend some extra time (our strategy worked!). Bono opened the dialogue by asking us where we were from. "Buffalo", we replied. "You drove all the way from Buffalo??", Bono exclaimed. At this point, I'm thinking, "All the way from Buffalo? First, it's only a 90 minute drive. Second, it's U2. Third, you're Bono and you're impressed that I made this journey?" Then Bono name-dropped someone he knew in Buffalo, which was especially amusing because usually we commoners name-drop celebrities, not the other way around. The name was Bruce Moser, and Bono was particularly excitable when he talked about his friend. "There's someone in Buffalo you've got to meet", he said. "His name is Bruce Moser, and he is an incredible guy. He was very important in helping U2 get their start in America." Turns out I already knew Bruce, and I had heard the story. Back in 1980 when U2 was touring America for the first time in support of their album, "Boy", Bruce – who was a record rep – not only promoted the show but let the fledgling Irish band stay at his house. That night at the show, the DJ in charge of introductions called them "V2". Bruce made it his mission to spread the gospel of U2 to Program Directors across the country, which he did to great success. To this day, although Bruce is no longer in the business, Bono always writes a Christmas card to Bruce and thanks him and his wife Mary from the stage whenever U2 plays Buffalo.

I went in thinking that meeting one of the biggest bands in the world would be a pompous, arrogant time – but to this day it remains the single greatest backstage experience of my life. How apropos that U2 would announce a 30th anniversary jaunt of "The Joshua Tree" the same year I'm releasing my book. Maybe this time I'll actually get to see it. At least I don't need to skip school.

CHAPTER 24

I'LL BE THE GREATEST PLANT OF YOUR LIFE

In the summer of 1998, my Pop Alternative station, Alice @ 92.9, held its first birthday concert at a club called The Funhouse in Buffalo and I booked the bands. The acts on the bill were Sister Hazel, Edwin McCain, Sister 7, and Kathleen Wilhoite. Kathleen was best known for her acting chops, most notably for playing Chloe on "ER". She had put out an album, which to this day is on one of my personal favorite Sunday morning playlists, and she opened the show. Sister 7, out of Austin, Texas, was a fun party rock band (not party rock like LMFAO, kids – party rock as in actual rock music that you party to). They had a mid-level hit called "Know What You Mean". The artist with the biggest hit - by far - at the time was Edwin McCain. You couldn't go anywhere that summer without hearing "I'll Be". But Edwin didn't want to headline, because it would be just him and his guitar whereas Sister Hazel was bringing their full plugged in band. I agreed to the order of the lineup and from the moment that night began, it was rare.

Kathleen came up and hugged me after she bounded off the stage. She told me it was the first time an audience sang her song back to her while she performed it. We played a track called "Symphony" and she was so excited that it connected in Buffalo. I wish she had more success on a national level, but her label V2 (which was Virgin founder Richard Branson's boutique imprint) did not have the promotional juice to make it happen. At the time, major labels controlled the charts – it would be another few years before Napster shook the labels' foundation and allowed smaller labels to make waves on a larger scale.

Sister 7 played a strong set, and then Edwin followed with his unplugged performance. I swear the joint shook when everyone sang the uber-catchy hook, "I'll be the greatest fan of your life". Upon Edwin's departure from the stage, he found me at the bar, put his arm around me and thanked me for the opportunity. I love this part of a Program Director's job description. Giving a shot to up and coming artists and having them show you appreciation brings me great joy. If you're Edwin McCain, you bring me great shots. Well, I don't know if they were great but they were hard liquor for sure. You name it – tequila, grasshoppers, kamikaze, Goldschlager – we drank it all. And when Sister Hazel came over to drink with us after the concert was over, that's when the real drinking began.

As it was a weeknight and I had to work in the morning – wait for it, I had to be at the station in the morning because Edwin was coming in to guest DJ – I declined Edwin's invitation to hop in his limo to go back to the hotel. Had I accepted the gesture, I would have seen Edwin McCain, Sister Hazel, and Sister 7 singing and playing the piano in the hotel bar to all hours of the night – paying the bartender to keep it open.

The next morning – and I know you're shocked – Edwin didn't show up to the station. His record rep called to apologize and tell me that he threw up in a ficus plant in the hotel lobby. Word had it the record label barred Edwin from ever performing with Sister Hazel again. A few years later in Detroit I saw Edwin backstage, and asked if he remembered that night in Buffalo. "The ficus plant", he said solemnly. "The ficus plant".

CHAPTER 25

DON'T BITE THE GOO THAT FEEDS YOU

When Bush, No Doubt, and the Goo Goo Dolls played HSBC Arena in Buffalo, it was a BFD. So much so that the Mayor of Buffalo declared it "Goo Goo Dolls Day" in the city, as the hometown boys were playing the arena for the first time. He presented the band with a key to the city on stage that night.

Years earlier I saw the Goo Goo Dolls at a club in Syracuse and it was intense. There was a mosh pit up front, the energy was palpable, and there was a sense that greatness was on its way. This proved to be true, as the song "Name" soared to the top of the pop charts that summer. That song broke the band and made the Goo Goo Dolls a household name. Now, what happens when a band like the Goo Goo Dolls has a mainstream pop hit is a return engagement to the same club 8 months later and a mosh pit that isn't so...moshing. A crowd filled with teenagers dropped off by their parents who stood in the back and sides of the room – somewhat indifferent, as they didn't know any of the songs. That is, until they played "Name" and the singalong began.

It's funny, really, how the Goo Goo Dolls started out as a hard rock band with mosh pits and ended up as an adult contemporary act for soccer moms but can you blame them? Saying someone "sold out" is so asinine. Who doesn't want to make money?

Back to Buffalo and we're guests of the record rep for the Goo Goo Dolls that night and the band is having a party after their set at a bar to celebrate the occasion. So after the Goos finished their performance, the rep told me where the party was and said, "Ready to go?" Problem was, Bush was a really hot band at the time and the other two people I was with really wanted to stay to watch the headliner. Frankly, I kinda wanted to watch the headliner. But when it is Goo Goo Dolls Day in their hometown, you really should go to their party. But I said no and we stayed for Bush. Never made it to the party. To this day, I feel bad about that because I'm sure the rep looked like a schmuck. He's supposed to be bringing the influential radio guy to the party and the guy stayed for the other band? In Buffalo?? That takes some brass and was arrogant on my part.

Over the years as I got older, I got better about taking care of the people who take care of me. Plus I realized how much more important the parties and mingling are than the show. While I still love live music, I've seen so many concerts that an open bar is now usually going to trump the music. And wouldn't you know it – even though I missed the soiree, the Goo Goo Dolls ended up just fine.

CHAPTER 26

CHINESE FOOD KARAOKE

I am a karaoke junkie. My addiction began in the early 1990's when I hosted a Friday Happy Hour at a bar called The Jukebox in Syracuse with the fabulous Cindy Ormond. I have sang karaoke hundreds of times and my go to number (everyone has to have a "go to" song) is Prince's "Kiss", which I belt out in falsetto. It always goes over particularly well because a) it's a relatively accurate version and b) because no one expects that voice to come out of my body. Of all the nights I've sang karaoke though, none was more entertaining than one summer evening in Buffalo, New York in 1999.

1999 was a great summer for me, which was unexpected because my Pop Alternative station had flipped format and now I was the Assistant Program Director and afternoon drive host of our country station while I worked out the rest of my contract and searched for my next job. With the pressures of Program Director and a struggling station behind me, I completely embraced my role at the country station. Named after a town in the Buffalo area, my airname was Ken Moore. While I was not a country music listener, I listened intently to the songs during my show, learned about the artists, and loved meeting the (very) loyal listeners. Plus, now that I wasn't a boss, I was spending more time with other employees of our radio group which led my wife and I to a happy hour at a bar in the Chippewa district one Friday afternoon with a bunch of great folks from the country station.

At some point in the evening (with already a fair number of drinks in us), we decided karaoke should be in order and we grabbed a copy of the free newspaper that listed events around town. It was in this publication that we discovered the VFW hall only a few minutes from where we were was hosting karaoke that night and we took this revelation as some sort of challenge. "The VFW!", we screamed. "Let's do it!" We figured karaoke at the VFW would be kitchy, a rite of passage of sorts. Down and dirty. Those were premonitions that proved to be right on all counts.

The VFW was dark, musty, and filled with people that had been drinking for a while. When one of us bellied up to the bar to buy the first round, it was discovered that beers were one dollar each. The next couple of hours were wildly fun. After singing a rendition of Alan Jackson's "Chatahoochee", a song I had only recently learned from playing it on the country station, a young man came right up to me and said (in an accent that can only be described as "Deliverance"), "You sang my favorite song. I want to sing with youuuuuu." Like I had a choice, I did a duet of "Friends in Low Places" with my new buddy. We sang country, rock, hip-hop, joined others in songs, while others joined us. It was awesome on all levels until a strange odor filled the windowless bar. "What's that smell?", John Paul asked. Everyone in the group wiggled their nose and strained their eyes just a bit, trying to determine the source of the smell. "Pizza?", someone guessed. "Tacos?", came another suggestion. "Wait. I know.", someone said. "That's Chinese food." It was at that moment that we saw a gentleman passed out on the floor near the front of the bar in a pool of spring rolls and sweet and sour pork. "Yep", I said. "Chinese food."

CHAPTER 27

CHRIS GAINES WAS HERE

In 1999, Garth Brooks (perhaps the most popular country singer on the planet) decided he wanted to try something else. He had nothing else to prove in the country arena. In fact, just a year earlier Garth traveled around the country doing something not heard of in touring lore – instead of playing one or two concerts in each city, he would play 7, 8, or 9 shows in each city. Garth's rationale was that he wanted to see America. Not the way most musicians get to see America, which is that every city and town and arena look exactly the same. The routine for most bands on tour is bus rolls into town, band goes to arena for soundcheck, band plays concert, band gets on bus to head to the next city. There is rarely time for the artists to actually spend quality time in the cities they visit. So Garth took advantage of his popularity to book a week or two of shows, and he'd sell out each and every show. We're talking about 20,000 seat arenas. In Minneapolis, Garth Brooks sold 159,000 tickets in four hours for a series of shows at the Target center from October 6-14, 1998. The month prior, he played six shows in Buffalo (one of which we attended), which was broadcast live during the CMA awards. Because Garth was spending a week or more in each city, he would constantly be spotted around town – at the bowling alley, a restaurant, a baseball game...it was exceptionally genius. Fun for him, and provided a jolt of free publicity in every city. Where would Garth show up next? Every radio station, country or not, would have a segment on Garth sightings. I also admired the fact that Garth was so in tune with his fans, he made sure the tickets were priced right ($17.50!) and t-shirts were around the same price. This was even more exceptional considering the Eagles were the first band to charge over $100 per ticket for their "Hell Freezes Over Tour" in 1994, and they sold out most of their shows. It's not that Garth couldn't charge and make much more, he just wanted to make sure that all his fans could afford it.

Fast forward to a year later. If Garth was stepping out of the box by setting up residencies in each city, he was really stepping out of the box when he created a fictional Australian rock star persona for himself named Chris Gaines. The idea was to make a fictional movie called "The Lamb" about Gaines, preceded by a pre-soundtrack titled "Garth Brooks in...The Life of Chris Gaines". There were plans to put out a soundtrack for the movie as well. Buzz was generated for the project with an episode of VH1's "Behind The Music", a guest hosting spot on Saturday Night Live, and an NBC special that aired on NBC on September 29, 1999 – one day after the pre-soundtrack was released. This special was taped at the NBC studios in Rockefeller Center and was pretty trippy (and I was there). Although Chris Gaines was essentially Garth in a straight-haired rockstar wig with blue highlights, Garth appeared as himself, talking about Chris Gaines who would be shown on a screen behind him. Garth told the story of Gaines' life – that he moved from Australia to L.A., was in a band called Crush, released his debut album in 1989, nearly died in a violent car crash...yeah. When he did perform songs from the album, he attempted to sound like an Aussie. The reception to the project was mostly one of "Huh???" The utter confusion and marketing bridges likely led to Garth abandoning the next phase of the project ("The Lamb" and its corresponding soundtrack) was never made and it was deemed a massive failure by many observers. That being said, the album was actually pretty decent, and the first single "Lost In You" was a Top 5 hit on the pop charts. This was his first and only U.S. Top 40 single. The album was certified double platinum in America which would have been a huge success for plenty, but not for a guy who just sold 159,000 tickets in 4 hours a year before. Stephen Thomas Erlwine of Allmusic believed the album would have been a much bigger success had it simply been released as Garth Brooks' first pop album, but we'll never know.

After the taping, we joined our friend Nick from Capitol Records at the Oak Bar at the posh Plaza (where we were staying). The Oak Bar opened in 1945 when it was owned by Conrad Hilton and once occupied the offices of E.F. Hutton (when we drink, people listen!). Naturally because it was dimly lit, had a 30 plus foot long oak bar and felt like the forties, we imbibed thematically. Martinis, Manhattans, Old Fashioneds, and Harvey Wallbangers, just because. Harvey Wallbangers because its fun to say, never mind the fact that we had no idea what was in it except that it was fruity and very, very strong. The night got very late and we may or may not have removed a sign from the Oak Bar upon our exit. This sign may or may not still be in someone's possession (it is not, however, in mine – unfortunately). Just the memories of an incredible evening.

CHAPTER 28

HOWARD STERN WORKED HERE, RIGHT?

When I first started working in Detroit, the radio station was located in the city near the river in an old house. That place had character and over the years was filled with characters. J Geils Band once played a concert up on the roof. When it was a country station, legions of artists that became mega stars walked the halls. And if you've ever seen the movie "Private Parts" and remember when Howard Stern wore a cowboy hat and worked very briefly at the country station in Detroit, that was W4 and the building I was now working in was the very same building Howard did his show in.

The only major difference between eras was that my office, which sat parallel to the studio separated by two way glass, used to be the studio. In other words, my office was once the studio in which Howard Stern worked. The city of Detroit doesn't exactly attract a great deal of international tourists, but since "Private Parts" came out in 1997 and this was 2000, the film was still a recent introduction into the pop culture universe.

One day while I was working on scheduling the music logs for the next day, three Japanese men showed up at my open door with cameras hanging from their necks. "This Howard Stern studio?", one of them asked. A giant smile filling my face and doing everything in my power to keep myself from laughing out loud, I said, "Yes, Howard Stern used to work here." The image of sheer delight spread across their faces, as they followed up with, "We take pictures, OK?" "Yes, ok", I told them, chuckling.

Those flash bulbs must have gone off a hundred if not a

thousand times. Pictures with one of them in it, pictures of all of them with me taking the shots, pictures with me in them. "Sank you very much", they said. "You are quite welcome", I replied and the only tourists that ever visited Alice 106.7 on Jefferson Avenue in Detroit made their way out the door to continue their trip.

CHAPTER 29

AWKWARD PROGRAM DIRECTOR MOMENTS

It is often said that being a radio station Program Director is more akin to being a babysitter than anything because the talent tend to need a lot of attention. Air personalities, while very creative, tend to be wildly insecure, have a deep seated fear of failure, and I'm fairly certain have a much higher percentage of ADD and ADHD employees than other industries. When you're dealing with people with eccentricities, strange things are bound to happen.

One of the more awkward ones was the DJ with a body odor problem. It was so bad that the room would fill up with an overwhelming stench within seconds of this person entering the room. The Program Director at the time (it was not me) knew about the issue but was trying to avoid dealing with it because, well, who wants to have that conversation? Ultimately the conversation was forced when the offender walked into the air studio and the DJ on duty vomited in the trash can. The Program Director expedited the discussion with the person, who did not even realize it was happening and it never happened again.

Another extremely awkward (and unfortunate) moment occurred in Buffalo when one of our DJs came back from a big concert at the arena by a popular hip hop artist. Although he was on air at our Pop Alternative station, he had a great affection for black music and culture. And he was white. The night of the concert, he came to the station excited as ever. Maybe too excited. He waltzed into the halls, and loudly exclaimed, "What's up my nig---!!" It must have been like the scene in Animal House when Boone yells out "Otis! My Man!" when the band stops and the entire bar filled with black people is staring at him. See, the radio station that was right next to ours in the hallway was an urban station and the employees there that night were African-American. The shout of joy from our employee did not go over terribly well.

I found out about the offense the next morning when one of the employees of the urban station complained. I was instructed, in no uncertain terms, to fire the DJ in question. After hearing the story and the sequence of events, I pleaded for his job to be saved. I know deep in my heart that he didn't have a racist bone in his body. To the contrary, he loved black people and hip-hop culture so much he had immersed himself in it so deeply he did not realize he had gone over an inappropriate line. You would be hard pressed to find someone that didn't judge people by the color of their skin more than this guy. But alas, the boss found himself in a difficult position and even though I argued that a warning or even a suspension would be warranted, termination was the decision. I was further dismayed that I was the one that had to tell him but that's how it went down. It was as miserable as I anticipated. He did not realize the mistake he had made but as I watched him squirm, head down and tears streaming, he pleaded for a suspension. Sadly, I had no choice but to let him go. At least I didn't have to ask for him to give me the station jacket off his back – I once had to call someone I fired from the same station and ask her to return the station ski jacket. She told me to fuck off.

There has perhaps been no stranger event I've dealt with than the "dropping trou" incident in Detroit. Next to the old house on Jefferson Avenue was a garage in which you found the headquarters of our company's sports station. One Sunday afternoon when one of my very young female part-time DJ's was doing her show in the house, an employee of the sports station showed up. According to the female DJ, he had been trying unsuccessfully to get her to go on a date with him. On this particular afternoon, he positioned himself in the middle of the room while she was on the air, dropped his pants, and proceeded to pleasure himself right in front of her. If that weren't enough, he finished the job before pulling his trousers back up, leaving the evidence in question right there in the middle of the carpet. When this poor girl was embarrassingly telling me the story that next day, she showed me the clearly fresh stain. Dealing with this situation was unpleasant on many levels, not the least of which was the fact that he wasn't terminated immediately. Eventually he was let go and hopefully got some help for his issues.

CHAPTER 30

THE GREATEST BACKSTAGE PARTY EVER...BUT DON'T EAT THE SUSHI

While I was in Buffalo at Alice @ 92.9 in the late 90's, we played Barenaked Ladies music. A LOT of Barenaked Ladies music. This made all kinds of sense, since BNL broke out of Toronto. Since you can hear Toronto stations in Buffalo, it was one of the first successful American markets for the band (as were other border towns, like Detroit). While in between BNL albums, bassist Jim Creeggan and his brother Andy (an early but now former member of BNL) were putting out music and touring behind their jazzy side project, Brothers Creeggan. Brothers Creeggan scheduled a concert at an awesome jazz club in downtown Buffalo called The Tralf and I was more than happy to help promote it.

This meant a lot to Jim Creeggan. As you might imagine, they didn't have Pop Alternative Program Directors banging down their doors begging to promote a jazz duo. Plus, this was a few years before BNL would release "One Week", the song that rocketed them to "A" level in the United States. So Jim Creeggan called to thank me for my support, and I told him that I was really looking forward to the show.

As you might know, it snows a little bit in Buffalo, New York. When time came for the show date, the conditions were such that the brothers were not going to make it down the Thruway into town and it had to be postponed. Jim called the station that afternoon and personally apologized to the fans (this is not a regular thing musicians do) and said the wait wouldn't be long before they came to play again. The date was rescheduled, we promoted the show and gave away more tickets. On the afternoon of the day of the rescheduled show, my phone rang. It was Jim. "You're not going to believe this, Jay", he told me. "They're not letting us across the border. We're apparently missing some work visa information and we don't have time to go all the way back to Toronto to get it and make the show. There's just no way. I am so sorry." He really was sorry, and we kept in touch over the next few months.

Fast forward a few years later to my employment at Alice 106.7 in Detroit, when our parent company AM/FM flew Program and Promotion Directors out to Los Angeles for company meetings (boy, those were the days). The first night of the conference, we were treated to a private party featuring a live performance by, yes, The Barenaked Ladies. After the show, the band was walking around introducing themselves when Jim Creeggan shook my hand. "Hi, I'm Jim." "Hi, Jim, I'm Jay", I replied back. Creeggan did a double take on my voice, tilted his head and asked, "Are you Jay Nachlis?" I earned instant cred points from the Directors around me when it was discovered that I'd been recognized by a Barenaked Lady. Creeggan and I had a very nice conversation and we exchanged cell phone numbers.

On the tour for "Maroon" that summer, a two-night stand in Detroit's outdoor Pine Knob Music Theater was the last stop after nearly a year of touring. As I didn't have tickets for the show, I took a chance and called my new friend Jim Creeggan on his cell phone and left a message. He called back within the hour. "Jay! How many tickets do you need?", he asked. "I'd love 4 if possible". "No problem", he told me. "I'll leave them for you at will call."

My Promotions Director Shelley, and my father-in-law Fred (who also lived in the Detroit area) accompanied my wife and I to the show. At the box office, we were surprised to see that 4 backstage passes were left in an envelope in addition to the tickets. The seats were stellar, 10th row center. The show was superb as usual, and after the show we made our way to the backstage area where we were greeted by a sight never seen before or since by these eyes at any backstage meet and greet. There was, for starters, a hot tub. With members of the Barenaked Ladies in it. There was a karaoke machine and a karaoke host. There was a sumo wrestling ring and suits if you were so inclined. There was every kind of alcoholic beverage you would ever want. And there was sushi. Rows and rows of sushi. Naturally, our first move was to help ourselves to the sushi – but one slight move to the unagi caused a guy dressed in black with an important looking laminate and a ponytail to throw his hand out. "No!", he scolded. "The sushi", he instructed, "is for the band only."

The next 2 ½ hours were an insane delight. Getting loaded with the Barenaked Ladies and my father-in -law. My Promotions Director hooking up with a roadie that was there with the opening band, The Proclaimers. Singing karaoke and being told "Great job" by the bassist for Barenaked Ladies. Getting lost looking for the car because we were there so late, the venue turned off all the lights in the parking lots. It was just a fantastic night – I just wish we had been able to try the sushi.

CHAPTER 31

OF COURSE THAT'S MY REAL NAME

Most radio personalities do not use their real names. When I arrived on campus at Syracuse University and started work at Z89, I intended to use "Jumpin' Jeremy Nachlis"! Fortunately I was talked out of that option by the Z89 Program Director at the time. Electing to go with a slick approach, I shortened Jeremy to Jay, but spelled it "J." and used the surname "Diamond". Thus my first airname ever used on a radio station was J. Diamond, and it was the start of my new nickname – "Jay" – taking shape.

When I was hired for weekend overnights at Y94FM in Syracuse, I was encouraged to be "real" and "genuine", which led me to use "Nachlis" on air for the first time, combined with the informal "J." The problem with J. Nachlis, as I learned within a short span, was the annunciation issue that surfaces when you verbalize the end of "Jay" and the start of "Nachlis". It was most notably brought to light when the station got me my first jock shout. A jock shout is a vocal jingle of sorts, in which a group of people shout your name. When played on air, the jock shout is followed by a station jingle, which then plays into a song. The problem? My jock shout sounded like "(shouted) Jaaaane Atlas!! (sung) Y94fm!" Listeners would actually call the request line and refer to me as "Jane", which was not exactly positive reinforcement of my manhood. Ultimately I decided not to change it, and lived with the "Jane" thing for a total of four years, from part-time status all the way up to Assistant Program Director and Afternoon Drive Air Talent.

Although I was not on-air full time at K101 in San

Francisco, I did host the wildly popular "Saturday Night Disco Show" as J. Diamond. Even with very big ratings on Saturday night (if there's anywhere a disco show should work, it would be San Francisco), it would be eventually cancelled by the company's format Vice President who felt it didn't "fit the format."

Next it was onwards to Buffalo's Alice @92.9 in 1997, where I adopted an airname that one of my cohorts at Z89, Brian Lapis, had – "Jefferson". I liked this name for two reasons. First, it was one name. Although I'd sometimes get the one name chuckle: "Like Cher or Madonna!", it was, in fact, easy to remember and perhaps the antithesis of a name like Jay Nachlis. Second, I thought it was cool. When Alice/Buffalo flipped formats, I ended up doing shifts at stations all over the building and I used different airnames for all of them. I found it fun to come up with the various names targeted for the format and went super cheesy just for the hell of it. On the Jammin' Oldies station, I used "Otis Day". On the country station, I split the name of a Buffalo suburb, Kenmore, into "Ken Moore".

On to Detroit, where the redux of "Jefferson" was divine intervention – inspired by the moment I was taken to the radio station for the first time on the city's Jefferson Avenue. Like the merging of two towns in Buffalo, I fused the street name that was the home of the station – Jefferson – with one of the most famous streets that cut through the Motor City, Woodward Avenue. So for my time in Detroit, although I was not on air very often, when I was...I was Jefferson Woodward.

The best decision I made in Raleigh was the decision I made regarding one of my first ideas for an airname. I had recently seen "Gladiator" in the theater and loved it. I thought it would be memorable to adopt the name "Maximus". I enjoyed the irony of the name as well, since I'm not exactly of a Maximus build. As it happened though, on one of those first days in Raleigh I was taken to lunch by my boss to a restaurant called Foster's in Cameron Village. When I went to pick up some beer at the grocery store, I made subtle note of the fact that Foster's was on special. When I drove around that evening, I passed Foster's Auto Body on Capital Boulevard. Thus, I chose Foster as my airname in Raleigh. My only regret was that I didn't use Foster Child from the get-go. As Curtis Media President Phil Zachary once noted, "You could have used the sweeper, 'Foster Child. Are you my parents?' It could have been your tag line!"

CHAPTER 32

THE CITY THAT NEVER SLEEPS – BUT OFTEN RICKSHAWS

One of the benefits of working for Clear Channel was that they owned the promotion company for nearly every concert and Broadway show. You could purchase tickets directly through them, and although you aren't given a discount you are guaranteed very good seats that are held for that purpose. When Molly Ringwald was starring in "Cabaret" on Broadway in the renovated Studio 54, my wife and I planned a trip to New York City and bought our tickets through Clear Channel.

Our hotel was about 15 long blocks away from the venue. Too long to walk, but a relatively short cab ride. When we emerged from the lobby at 7:20pm en route to the 8pm curtain, we figured we had plenty of time to spare and even time to enjoy a cocktail at the theater bar before the show began. As it happens, despite the sea of yellow cabs in New York City, it is very difficult to get one on a Friday evening at 7:20. Or 7:30. Or 7:35, which is when we started really freaking out because we were going to miss the beginning of the show. You know how it goes – if you miss curtain, you're SOL for at least 15 minutes and often longer than that if not the entire first act. As we had paid $85 per ticket, that was not a scenario we were prepared to face so we walked quickly.

A few blocks up, we found a hotel that did have cabs approaching to pick up patrons but the line wrapped around the establishment. There was no way we would get a taxi in time and running the entire way wasn't even an option because Jennifer was wearing heels and her feet were already killing her. That's when Jennifer spotted the rickshaw and a couple negotiating with the driver for a ride. Either I perceived the couple to be hemming and hawing or I wasn't thinking at all because I just rudely just walked in front of the couple and asked the driver, "Can you get us to Studio 54 in less than 15 minutes?" "Of course", was the response and we hopped in with no discussion of how much this jaunt was going to cost us (it didn't really matter at this point).

The ride was wild, exhilarating and even fun as the driver pedaled the bike furiously, weaving in and out of traffic through the streets of Manhattan. Now we were smiling, confident that we were in fact going to make it on time and as he directed the rickshaw off the street, up over a curb and hit the brakes just as we spotted Studio 54 on our right. "Wow", I said. "How much do we owe you?" He thought for a moment. "How does 15 bucks sound?" It sounded like a super NYC bargain to me as I handed the super-biker a twenty and instructed him to keep the change. When we made our way into the theater, wouldn't you know we even had time to get that 15 dollar cocktail at the bar before the show began. Our seats were at a table just two rows from center stage. The show was sweet. Somehow the rickshaw made it that much sweeter.

CHAPTER 33

9/11

When the first plane hit, I was at the light waiting to take a left turn onto Detroit's Jefferson Avenue. My wife called my cell phone and we discussed in a confused state, like so many of us were in at that moment. The news was speculating at first that it was a small plane. Terrorism wasn't the first thing that ran through our minds because, after all, flying a plane into the World Trade Center? That couldn't happen, could it? So we figured it must have been a small plane that made a terrible mistake, though we did consider the possibility that it was a terrorist with a small plane. It never even entered our minds that it could have been a commercial jet. Until, of course, I walked into the radio station, joined the others watching the coverage on the news, and saw the second plane hit the tower.

Everyone in America (and perhaps the world) remembers where they were when they heard about or watched the planes fly into the buildings. We vividly remember the image of the towers crumbling to the ground. The passage of time, though, has seemed to mute the memory of the other planes – and it was the other planes that affected my initial decision making on that day. If the event has been isolated to one plane flying into the World Trade Center, that would have been bad enough. If it had stopped at two planes, that would have been bad enough. But at least we would have known the World Trade Center was the only target, that it was somehow contained at that juncture. But then we heard a plane crashed into The Pentagon. A plane flew into the symbol of America's defense system? We couldn't stop that? After we learned that United 93 crashed in a Pennsylvania field on the way to

Washington and everyone speculated (correctly, as it would turn out) that the target was the White House, rumors ran rampant. Every plane was suspicious. We heard that a plane over Cleveland was unaccounted for. Cleveland? That's only a few hours from Detroit. What if it's coming here? We have nuclear facilities...I mean, these were our thought processes. Everything was unprecedented and without a roadmap. When you hear terrorists have crashed three commercial jets, they've brought down two of our tallest buildings in our biggest city, the Pentagon has a hole in it, the FAA is grounding all airplanes, and who the hell knows where our President is – well, I was going to go home.

I had no desire to be brave and go down swinging with my radio station. With a radio station? Don't get me wrong, radio plays an important role in emergencies. A crucial role. Local radio can keep you informed when all other sources have lost power (all you need is a battery!). But let's be honest. Who was coming to Alice 106.7 for their news on this day? If you weren't watching TV (which almost everyone was), you would have on a news station. "America's under attack, I think I want to hear some Nickelback." Ummm...no. Most importantly, while I love my job, my family simply comes first in my value system. So at this moment, on this day, I only wanted to be with my wife. The General Manager of the station was, in fact, in complete agreement with me. We could easily simulcast one of the local TV stations on our air and nobody would have to be at the station to operate it. Clear Channel corporate had sent an e-mail giving the blessing to its local stations to either simulcast the news station in the cluster if there was one (which there was not in our case) or a local TV station. I told Steve Black, our afternoon guy, that he did not need to come in that afternoon.

As Steve related this story publically years later, he says

there was no way he would stay home. He saw it as his responsibility as an air personality to be on the air for his listeners that day. Steve once worked with Ted Nugent on Uncle Teddy's morning show and his "call of duty" streak was similar to something you would hear from The Nuge. Black went on the air that afternoon and created great radio. He relayed the news as it happened, took requests for songs that people were feeling in the mood for in that moment, and played songs that meant something to him personally – emotions and song styles that changed by the minute. It was completely off script, but it was beautiful. It was a theme we continued the next day starting with our morning show and I'm proud of the work we did.

By the same token, I don't have any regrets for feeling the way I felt or for making the early decisions I did. Nothing in my life experiences comes close to what I felt that day and, truth be told, it made my job seem unimportant. I know it is important – I think over the next few months, our station provided an escape from the 24/7 dose of talking heads on the news. We were there with music, but we were also there to listen and go through the emotions together. That was the correct role to play. But on that day- on September 11th, 2001 – radio was unimportant to me. Family was the only important thing.

There was a Clear Channel memo that went out to its Program Directors that advised them what songs not to play in heightened sensitivity to the 9/11 tragedy. The company received heaping portions of criticism for the list, which included a vast swath of music that could be construed as insensitive. The songs included "Stairway To Heaven", "Jet Airliner", and "Only The Good Die Young". Looking back on that time, I was sensitive about playing those songs, as well as a great many others and I don't think that's anything to

apologize for. We were making it up as we went along –
seemingly every song seemed insensitive and brought up
troubling images. To paraphrase Tom Hanks as US Airways
"Miracle on the Hudson" pilot Chesley "Sully" Sullenberger,
nothing has precedent until it happens. We didn't know how
we would feel, react, or what we would do in that moment
because nothing like that moment had ever existed. All we
could do was make our best guesses and hope our judgment
was on the mark.

CHAPTER 34

LIFE IMITATES ART

In 2008, while I was Program Director and Afternoon Talent at 96rock in Raleigh, the movie "Animal House" was celebrating its 30th anniversary and that gave me an idea for a promotion. I envisioned holding a toga party at a local bar, just like in the film. There was a bar in Raleigh that was small (like the Dexter Lake Club), had a stage in front of a brick wall (like the Dexter Lake Club), and I had a friend with a band who agreed to play the role of Otis Day & the Knights. With permission secured from the bar for the promotion, the party was on.

The first step was creating a video featuring our favorite lines from "Animal House", which my morning show Salt and Demetri quarterbacked and posted on Youtube. The mother of one of the morning show interns baked a cake like the float in the movie (I know, it's a little strange to ask someone's mom to bake a cake that says "Eat Me", but she offered.) We invited listeners to join us in wearing togas to the party and my wife and I were getting ready to go out when I got the call that set an ominous tone for the evening. It was my friend with the band. "They're not going to let us go on.", he told me. What? It wasn't even 9pm, the start time for the event. "We can't sound check and they're saying we can't play down here, so we're leaving." Pump the brakes. "Whoa, whoa, hold on. First, who is saying this?", I asked, to which I found out it was the owner of the club. "OK, I'll be down there in a few minutes." We finished putting on our togas and rushed to the venue where there was all kinds of confusion.

The decision maker at the bar had decided that the band

could not go on until 11:30 because the noise would disrupt the comedy shows that were in progress in the club upstairs. He claimed he was told that the band was an acoustic trio – that he never would have approved a full band to play in his bar before 11:30pm. This was why my friend's band was not allowed to sound check when he called me earlier. The start time was a contentious issue and one I didn't feel we could negotiate on, since we had advertised a 9pm start time. I could deal with a 10pm start, but the event was billed as 9p-11p. 11:30 was well past when we were supposed to be done. Heated conversations were taking place around 9:30 when the band began to play and the boss stormed over to the stage and started unplugging cords from their equipment. The band's sound guy took an immense amount of umbrage to someone messing with his stuff and my friend jumped off the stage, prepared to come to the defense of his sound guy. A heated conversation had now escalated to fire, and I jumped into the fray. I reminded the owner (in as stern a manner as is possible while wearing a toga) that we had delivered on our promise of advertising his establishment and that he was falling short of his commitments to us. That's when he took it too far and personally insulted my friend and I could not take it anymore.

You have to understand that I am a very, very calm person under most circumstances. I'm not a red personality, I'm skilled at negotiating and handling disagreements, I don't often lose my cool, and I had never – ever – lost my cool with a client. I understand that I'm representing the company and I would never put that relationship in jeopardy. But when he insulted my friend after treating the rest of my employees like dirt that evening, I just lost it. I stared into his eyes and said, "You know what?" Here it comes. "You're an asshole." This guy's face turned beet red as we moved outside into the back alley, the giant warehouse-like door swung wide open so everyone could see and hear. "You don't know who I am!", he screamed. He threatened to call the president of our company and have me fired. He told me he was cancelling all his advertising on all our stations and that I was going to lose my job. "Our company doesn't want to do business with assholes like you.", I spat back. I'm fairly certain no one has ever talked to him like that – except, perhaps, when he was a kid long before he was able to finance his Napoleon complex. "Get out. All of your people out. You're on my property. I'm calling the police.", he said. "Fine", I said, as I walked off and fired one parting shot. "Fuck you." I was honestly on a different level of emotion, one I'd never felt before. I had no concerns of repercussion, because I felt so right in how I was acting. I didn't even feel like it was me talking. I did call my General Manager that night and told him what was going on and the next couple of days spent great lengths of time on the phone describing each detail of the event to the company's president and our GM as it was the weekend. Nothing like getting your Sunday interrupted by this kind of event.

Soon after we were kicked out, we walked next door to another client of the station, a country bar where the owner welcomed us filling his deck with a large group of people wearing togas. Moments later the police did arrive, but we were now off his property despite the fact that we could see them from where we were. I hated putting my company in that position and sure enough, he cancelled all his advertising. In fact, he refused to do business with our company right until the day he sold it. My highest admiration goes to my superiors at my company, who defended me at every turn. Not only did they not submit to his demands to fire or even put me on double secret probation, the event was put quickly in the rear view mirror never to really be spoken of again. I think they knew I would never have acted that way unless I felt provoked and that it wasn't going to happen again.

Now it is pretty amusing to look back at an Animal House Toga Party promotion that turned into something perhaps even crazier than a night at Delta House itself. Fat, drunk and stupid is no way to go through life, son.

CHAPTER 35

THE TWO GREATEST PROMOTIONS WERE THE SAME PROMOTION

It doesn't take long for one to realize the significance of hockey in Detroit, Michigan. There is the "Hockeytown" logo on the ice at Joe Louis Arena. The Hockeytown Café is in downtown Detroit. Gordie Howe is revered as much as any athlete, anywhere. It is generally not an easy task to get a ticket to see the Detroit Red Wings play. Good radio Program and Promotion Directors look to create promotions around something the town is already talking about so that interest in the promotion is virtually guaranteed. It was therefore a no-brainer to create a promotion around the Red Wings, while I was Program Director at Alice 106.7 in Detroit, when they prepared to take on the Carolina Hurricanes in the 2002 Stanley Cup Finals.

My brainchild was a "mobile greeting card". The idea of having listeners sign giant greeting cards was nothing new. Christmas time? Bring a giant greeting card to the mall for listeners to sign that you send to the troops overseas. A big hurricane has struck somewhere? Clothing drive and a giant greeting card. The mobile greeting card I envisioned, however, would be the car itself that we would deliver in person to the Carolina Hurricanes. It was brash, cocky, and arrogant. Not far removed from sending a giant middle finger to Raleigh. Yes, this was a promotion that was quite right for the Motor City.

The first step was to get a car, and we didn't have much time. But the company did have relationships with many car dealerships around town that were advertisers. We didn't know exactly the kind of car we wanted, but we knew it should be old and a little junky, especially since we were going to junk it up with traces of Sharpie all over it. In Detroit, a promotion involving a foreign car is not an option. We called our contacts at the dealerships to see what used cars they had on the lot that they might be willing to trade for mentions.

"Trade for mentions" is exactly what it sounds like. A barter between a radio station and a company in exchange for goods or services where no cash changes hands. The value of the promotion would be in the tens of thousands of dollars, and the kind of car we were looking for surely wouldn't exceed five or six thousand in value so this would be a good deal for the dealership.

The call came in to the General Manager, who relayed the news. "It's a 1993 Chrysler New Yorker Fifth Avenue. Do we want it?" Did we want it? This wasn't going to be just a mobile greeting card now, this was a pimp mobile. This was "Look out North Carolina, Detroit is up in this bitch". It was perfect and awesome in every way...except that it was green. It had to be in the Red Wings colors, which were red and white. We had a very short turnaround and had to get it painted that weekend. Turned out the executive assistant at our company had a son who owned an automotive repair shop and even though painting wasn't exactly part of his business model, he was happy to donate his time and materials to get it painted red.

Once the base paint job was completed, the real fun began. We gathered the troops down to the front of the station on Jefferson Avenue and began decorations. Since this was a mobile greeting card, the first order of business was to come up with the greeting – and "HURRICANES BLOW" sounded as good a greeting as any to me. The rest of the white spray paint was used for other messages, like "Go Wings" and of course some self-promotion was in order so Alice 106.7 was scrawled in a few places around the vehicle. My wife's contribution was to make miniature Stanley Cup replicas out of aluminum foil, which we placed strategically around the car. The coup de'tat was a larger version, which became the defacto hood ornament. The octopus has an important place in Detroit Red Wings playoff lore (they are sometimes thrown on the ice during games, which will get you ejected from Joe Louis Arena), so we procured a few stuffed octopii for additional car décor. There were colorful streamers and the like to add some flair.

Once the decoration process was complete, we set up "signing stops" around the Detroit area where listeners could stop by and autograph the car with black sharpies. We selected high traffic areas around town, including malls and restaurants. The signing stops were the largest and most successful remotes I'd ever seen. Over the course of the week, hundreds of Detroiters made their way to the signing stops to write their names and good luck messages (and often insults for Hurricanes fans) on the car. It's funny – despite the fact that Detroit is probably the American city most often unfairly stereotyped as the wasteland of the country, residents of the Motor City have no issues throwing the hick stereotyping of the south at North Carolina. I think citizens of Hockeytown were a little indignant that Raleigh even had a team ("Hockey doesn't belong in the south!"). An interesting side storyline was that a Detroiter, Compuware founder Peter Karmanos, owned the Hurricanes. Publicity for our venture was helped by a piece that the local ABC TV affiliate filmed, when we elected to remove all songs that had to do with Hurricanes from our music rotation. I was filmed in our studio, flinging CDs across the room, from long and short range, sometimes behind my back, while shouting, "Rock You Like A Hurricane? OUT!" CD hits the trash can. "Rain King? GONE!" Thump.

Even revered Detroit legend Bob Seger wasn't exempt from this publicity stunt. "Against The Wind? SEE YA!" Bang. The convergence of the car stunt and song stunt resulted in tremendous exposure for our station. In Cinderella fashion, despite losing the first game, the Wings went on to stomp the Hurricanes and won the Stanley Cup.

Our afternoon guy Steve Black drove the car to Raleigh and parked it in front of the arena. When he did call-ins back to the station, he was amazed at the reaction of Hurricanes fans. "They are the nicest people I've ever met", he said. "They are incredibly welcoming and are really curious about what we're doing." Can you imagine what would have happened had a radio station in Raleigh sent a car with Detroit insults and parked it in front of the Joe? (Hold that thought). Naturally the car, returned safe and sound back to Detroit, rolled down Woodward in front of a million plus people for the victory parade. It was the greatest promotion I'd ever attempted until....

Spring 2006. My Raleigh radio station, 96rock, was preparing for a music and branding shift. The station was going to evolve from an alternative leaning rock position in the market to a broader, more mass appeal rock position that would incorporate 4 decades of rock n roll with a new accompanying slogan – "Everything That Rocks". There was only one problem – the Carolina Hurricanes were marching through the playoffs and getting close to reaching the Eastern Conference finals. We knew that any new branding message we tried to expose on the air ("Hey, did you hear 96rock is now playing everything?") would be engulfed by what was clearly the talk of the town ("Did you see that Canes game last night?") That's when Phil Zachary came up with the insanely inspired idea to leverage the hype of the Hurricanes to push through our new message. This little dose of genius was called

"96.1 The Cup".

The idea for 96.1 The Cup was born in Phil's office on a Friday afternoon. That next morning, my staff and I met around a table at a local coffee shop and brainstormed ideas for imaging. We wrote short sweepers to go between songs, long "attitude sweepers", music promos, sweepers with inserts for listeners. There was a new logo and website that our webmaster would design, as he registered the domain 961thecup.com that day. There were banners to be ordered to take to 96.1 The Cup events – because until the Hurricanes either won the Stanley Cup or were eliminated from the playoffs, 96rock was now going to be known as 96.1 The Cup, playing "Championship Rock". That tagline was the way to introduce the broader music mix to the audience – so many of the songs we were adding to the playlist were great sports anthems anyway. Somehow, all the material was written, voiced by our voice talent in Pittsburgh, and produced and put in to start that Monday morning. Oh, and there was something else. I had an idea for the perfect promotion to supplement 96.1 The Cup. We just needed to get a car.

Again, somehow within hours that Friday afternoon, our sales team procured an old Ford Crown Victoria and once again, Phil struck again with a name – instead of the Crown Vic, the car would be referred to as the "Cane Vic". We had no time to get it painted, nor did we have any connections to do so – therefore it was my purchase of 18 cans of red spray paint at Carquest Auto Parts that became the base of the Cane Vic – painted by me and my team in the parking lot of the Carolina Ale House near the station. Since this paint was really more of a touch up product, the car didn't look nearly as polished and smooth as the Detroit version. It looks rough and ragged, which my team loved. The next step, like in Detroit, was to take the Cane Vic to signing stops around town and despite the fact that Raleigh is no hockey town, they were wildly successful. People ate it up. This time we did it without the help of any TV news coverage (a competing radio company owns the CBS and Fox affiliates in town, which makes it tricky to get promotional coverage on their newscasts). The NBC affiliate graciously offered to partner with us on the promotion, in which case we would have received plenty of TV coverage. Our concern was that this was our promotion. Our idea. We didn't want to share it and make it look like a dual situation – and I'm glad we made that decision.

The "Cane Vic" promotion led up to the Eastern Conference finals against the Buffalo Sabres which was one of the greatest 7-game series in hockey history. Evenly matched with speed and youth, the series went down to the wire with the Hurricanes pulling out Game 7 and advancing to the Stanley Cup finals against the Edmonton Oilers. During the Sabres series, our midday jock Crash drove the car to Buffalo, where he got a great deal of coverage – appearing on the Shredd and Ragan morning show on 103.3 The Edge as well as multiple TV stations. We were somewhat amazed that the car was not destroyed in Buffalo – many Sabres fans in Raleigh were belligerent and even violent at the RBC Center – and it would not have been surprising if they took out their anger on our mobile insult card in their town. In fact, we had considered and prepared for that possibility in getting Crash home. Fortunately it was not an issue.

That doesn't mean the Cane Vic wasn't destroyed – it was. By Carolina Hurricanes fans following the Game 7 Stanley Cup Finals win over Edmonton. I suppose it was appropriate – it was their car, their promotion, and their ending. And what a promotion it was.

CHAPTER 36

NEVER TRUST A GROWN MAN WITH A PONYTAIL

Soon after I started as Program Director at 96rock in Raleigh, 3 Doors Down was playing a show at a 2,000 plus capacity dive bar-style concert hall. Radio stations are required to ask permission from the concert promoter, record label, or both to broadcast from the venue for a show. This permission usually ultimately comes from artist management. In the case of 3 Doors Down, it came down to the day of the show and either we were still waiting for permission or...I forgot to ask. Either way, I decided to send my DJ and promotions team to the venue to do the afternoon show live.

They set up as they normally would, with the tent, table, and microphones and Marti antenna sending a signal from the truck. Mere minutes into the broadcast, my cell phone rang. It was our afternoon host. "They're telling us to get off the property", he tells me. "What?", I responded. "We play more 3 Doors Down than any other station in the market." He was firm. "I know, I told him", my jock told me. "He says we have to go." Knowing that the radio station was located only 3 minutes from the venue, I instructed, "Wait. Don't do anything. I'm coming over there."

When I rolled up to the venue, my promotions team was already packing up the broadcast. "What are you doing?", I said. At that moment, a guy representing the promoter gets right up in my face and says, "Are you the Program Director?" "Yes", I tell him. He saddled up on his high horse for a nice long ride. "You just made a rookie mistake", he tells me. "You can't be here without permission. What a bush league rookie mistake." Blown away by his attitude, I wanted so badly to say "Do you know who the fuck I am? I'm Jay mother fuckin Nachlis and I just moved here from the Motor City. Major Market, bitch. You ever been to a Top 10 market, asshole?" But I didn't, because that's not me. That's my interior voice – I just happen to have that filter in the brain that stops it from getting to the mouth. I simply whipped out my phone, called the record label rep, and within minutes had permission for us to broadcast inside the venue. I won that battle, and fortunately I never had to deal with that guy again.

That guy had a ponytail.

CHAPTER 37

GETTING KICKED OUT OF AN AWARDS SHOW

I didn't exactly get kicked out of the Billboard Music Awards in Las Vegas. I just wasn't invited back.

The Billboard Awards setup was much like the Grammys, in that there were two days of doing your show live from a backstage area. Because the Billboard Awards was held in the MGM Grand, the radio stations were set up in a ballroom at the hotel. Since the show was live for afternoon drive on the east coast, we were live from Noon-4pm pacific time. The network that broadcast the show was responsible for producing the radio shows. They saw it as an opportunity to promote their shows. So, there were the really incredible interviews, like the time I asked Smokey Robinson if he thought Michael Jackson was guilty (he didn't). Or the time I sang the "Chips" theme with Erik Estrada. Or the time I interviewed Motley Crue not long after their reunion with Vince Neil. But for every great interview opportunity, there were three crappy offerings, like the one with the "star" of "Joe Millionaire" (he swore live on air). The network was paying a lot of money for the radio stations to come out, so I understood the obligation to do the interviews and help promote their shows.

On the morning of the second broadcast day, we were to be shown a screener of a new show that was making its premiere called "Bones". This was a mandatory screening because we would be required to interview author Kathy Reichs that day, whose books the show was based on. I was in attendance and was watching (and enjoying) the show when my cell phone rang and I saw it was my boss on the caller ID. I quietly walked to the other side of the room, where I learned it was both my immediate boss and the president of our company on the phone. They had something they needed to cover with me and I spent the next 20 minutes on that call.

When I creeped back over to my table, a network higher-up gave me a fairly evil looking stare but I didn't think much of it at the time. My show began at Noon, and indeed one of the interviews that day was with Kathy Reichs. It was an enjoyable interview, one that even inspired her to say, "That was the best interview of the day. You clearly watched the show." "Thank you", I replied, not realizing we would meet again later that evening.

The second meeting with Reichs took place at Studio 54, a club inside the MGM Grand where the Billboard Awards pre-party was taking place. Kathy was there with her daughters and, as fate would have it, one of her daughters was there with a guy from Raleigh. The earlier interview and the Raleigh connection made for an easy in with their group, and we had an awesome time which continued when one of the Reichs daughters invited me to dinner with their group. I accompanied them and completed the evening over a lovely steak.

When I returned to Raleigh after what I felt was a banner trip, I learned the network supervisor had called one of my superiors to complain about me. I left a mandatory screening and therefore had not followed protocol. I was told to write an apology letter with an explanation of what happened. She even threatened to stop buying commercials on the station because of the incident. Fortunately it did blow over and they are a terrific client, although I was never invited back to a Billboard Music Awards.

The best thing, however, to come out of the Billboard trip experience was when I called that guy I met from Raleigh a few weeks later to meet up for lunch. Sam and I are best friends to this day.

CHAPTER 38

CANCER.

Noah Wolfson was one of my best friends growing up in San Francisco. In elementary school through middle school, we were as thick as thieves. When we turned 14, Noah and I went to different high schools and, as happens often when this happens, we drifted apart. This was around the time Noah was diagnosed with leukemia.

While Noah fought leukemia, I was mostly out of the picture. He missed a great deal of school while fighting the illness, and I was no longer in his circle of friends. But a couple of years later, the phone rang and it is a conversation that haunts me to this day. "Jeremy", Noah said in a weak, raspy voice. "I'm dying. I want to see all my friends and I really need you right now. Can you come over to the house this Saturday?" I'm not sure how much of being 15 you remember, but it's generally not the most empathetic time in one's life. The things that seem so darn important to a 15 year old are often the most trivial when one looks back years later. Dances. Relationships. What clothes to wear, music to listen to, parties, what your room looks like. The basketball team. But death? Death was not something I had confronted yet and I was not prepared.

I had a young mother who gave birth to me at 17 and therefore had very young grandparents who were barely in their 60s at the time. Besides my Uncle Steven, who has lived his entire adult life with a chronic illness, nobody close to me had a serious illness much less died. My children, ages 12 and 9 at the time of this writing, have already been to three funerals in their lifetime. But in 1988 at age 15, I had not been to one.

My response sounded sincere and I'm sure I meant it at the time. "Yeah, I'll be there", I told Noah. But even talking to him made me feel uncomfortable and the thought of going to see him days before his death was daunting. What would I say? Why did he want me there anyway? We hadn't spoken in years. I thought about it a great deal that day but managed to do the teenager thing and shelved it in some mental file cabinet far, far away. This, of course, meant that when Saturday arrived, I didn't show up. It wasn't until 24 years later that I would find out I wasn't the only one.

Noah's father, Phil Wolfson, is a psychiatrist in the San Francisco Bay Area and is still acquaintances with my mother. Through this relationship I learned that Phil was writing a book about Noah and in the summer of 2011, my mom arrived in Emerald Isle, NC for our annual beach trip with a signed copy of the book. "Noe".

In the book, which only took me about a day and a half to read, I learned how the struggle of Noah's illness had torn apart Phil and his wife Alice, leading to an inevitable separation. I discovered how, at first, Noah didn't accept the diagnosis and was miserable to the hospital staff – often flailing and screaming and making it exceedingly difficult for them to treat him. I found out that, once he decided he was determined to live, he fought until the end – even undergoing an extremely painful experimental treatment with a very low success rate that required him to live in isolation, away from his family, in another state. I learned how in those final weeks of life, Noah, who had a deep love for swimming, was hell bent on getting in the pool just one more time – and he tried unsuccessfully as the water was way too cold for his very sensitive body temperature. I think about how awful he must have felt – the frustration he must have been going through –

to not be able to enjoy just one more moment doing something he loved so much. I wondered, of course, if there would be any sort of mention of me and, while I'm not mentioned by name, an incident is mentioned in the book that is worse than any individual mention. Much worse. Phil describes, in great deal, how Noah had in fact called many friends from over the years and invited them to show up that Saturday. Noah was excited to see his friends just one more time before he passed on from this world. He wanted to tell his friends not to worry about him when he is gone – that he'll be ok.

Nobody showed up. Not one.

I had already been living with the guilt of not being there for Noah when he needed me most, but finding out that every friend had abandoned him in his darkest, most terrifying hours – on the doorstep of death – brought me to uncontrollable tears for quite some time. Phil writes in "Noe" that he hoped people would remember him but didn't think they would. In the fall of 2000, I began a mission that ensured he'd never be forgotten and a never ending personal journey that would hopefully provide some karmic revitalization.

In the fall of 2000, I was the Program Director of Alice 106.7 in Detroit when Children's Miracle Network approached the station to see if we were interested in becoming their flagship station in the Motor City. Although I knew of CMN, I was not aware that they partner with stations nationwide to raise money for a specific children's hospital in that particular city. Beaumont was the CMN hospital in Detroit, and I saw this as a timely opportunity.

Truthfully, my initial motivations were selfish – or at least motivated by what was good for the radio station. We had recently flipped formats from country – a heritage station called W4 – and had debuted a new morning show, Davis and

Darla. I saw a partnership with CMN as an opportunity to align the station with a worthy charity (and nothing is more worthy than children). Plus, I envisioned Mark Davis and Darla Jaye anchoring the entire radiothon, which would help accelerate their brand name in the marketplace and paint them as caring members of the community. On Day 1 of the three day fundraising event, I showed up at the mall to begin our broadcast at 6am and there was a little problem. We couldn't get on the air.

Every telethon and radiothon has a phone bank and Children's Miracle Network had to order the phone lines from a local Detroit area phone company. There were rows and rows of phones, rows and rows of volunteers ready and willing to take donations, and when Davis and Darla went on the air that morning at 6am, we waited with baited breath for those phones to ring and ring.

But the phones didn't ring. Not one.

Not after 10 minutes, 15 minutes, or 30 minutes. At this point a great measure of self-doubt began creeping in. "Ok", I thought to myself. "I know this is our first radiothon and I know Davis and Darla haven't been on the air very long and I know it's early in the morning. But is it really conceivable that after a half hour, not one phone would ring?" I consulted with the on-site representatives from Children's Miracle Network, who confirmed they'd never seen anything like this at any radiothon anywhere – which further reinforced my self-doubt. Maybe I was a bad Program Director. Perhaps I'd promoted it wrong. It just had to be something I did.

Unless the problem was with the phones.

The CMN people who had set up the phone bank started calling the phone company's customer service center and calls to their customer service center at that hour of the morning were not yielding rapid results. There was a lackadaisical attitude on their part and, although they could confirm the lines on the phone bank were dead, there was nothing they could do – because the office hadn't yet opened. There was not a tech available to come fix it. We pleaded, we asked to be transferred to someone of higher authority, but the answer kept coming back the same – there was nothing they could do until after 9am. Considering that we were there to raise money for sick kids and every moment we were not on the air was a missed opportunity for money, it was a terrible way to start. So I took matters into my own hands.

Children's Miracle Network provides a great deal of training for the personalities that host their radiothons – so, although this was my first event for them, I had been ingrained with many of the basic tenets of a successful event by the extremely talented consultant Steve Reynolds. One of these tenets was to be natural and speak from the heart because listeners respond when they feel an emotional connection. To this point in my radio career, I had no opportunity to share heartfelt emotion, because let's face it – when I was on the air at music stations, I almost never talked for more than thirty seconds at a time. When I did talk, it wasn't exactly earth-shattering material. I delivered the call letters and a liner or the slogan – "Y94FM, with 50 minutes of music every hour". I'd introduce a song, talk about a contest, mention a pop culture event or a concert coming to town. It wasn't as easy as I'm making it sound, but it wasn't brain surgery either. Unless you're hosting a morning show or are on a talk station, opportunities to speak from the heart don't come about very often. But this was my first radiothon, I wanted to raise a ton of money in memory of my friend Noah, and the phone company had screwed it up and wasn't cooperating. So I stepped on to the staging area, asked Davis and Darla for the microphone, and said something like this:

"This has been one of the most rewarding months of my life getting ready for this radiothon. The countless hours that we've spent putting this event together has made us stronger as a team, and I can't thank the volunteers enough for all they've done. Everyone here is a volunteer. Our friends from the mall, Children's Miracle Network, and the men and women that made sure they were here on time this morning so they could answer the phones and take your donations. But guess what? The phones don't work. Children's Miracle Network set up the installation of these phone lines weeks ago and today – this morning – as we've been asking you for your donations to help sick children, we've watched as the phones have remained silent. And I thought to myself – is it possible that Alice 106.7 listeners are just not as generous as I thought they were? Maybe times are just so tough out there that nobody is able to call in? But we discovered that in fact the phone lines were installed improperly. So we called the phone company. And do you know what they told us? They said they can't do anything until regular business hours. Well you know what? (At this point, my face was red and I was literally shaking). Apparently you don't care about sick children. Apparently it's more important for you to keep bankers hours than it is to fix a problem you caused. Because since our volunteers – that gave up their precious time- haven't been able to answer the phones to take donations, we've potentially lost thousands of dollars since we started this radiothon at 6 this morning. So fix this problem, or everyone in Detroit is going to know what a miserable company you are. Shame on you. Shame on you."

Then I dropped the mic on the floor like I was Eminem finishing off a freestyle battle at The Shelter in "8 Mile". (Not planned – my emotions had so completely taken over that I'm not even sure I heard what I was saying or doing). I lost all concern about the implications this rant would have on my job, or how our company – AM/FM - would react to one of its employees insulting one of the largest employers in the state of Michigan and one of the biggest advertisers on our stations.

Within minutes, someone reached the CMN rep and told her that a tech was on the way to fix the problem. By 8:30 they had fixed the issue, but at that point we had lost two and a half hours of fundraising. From that point forward, we used the issue as the key to our plea – now that the phones are working, we need you to please donate now to help us make up for all the money we lost during the valuable morning hours when listeners are on the way to work. Did Alice 106.7 listeners respond? Did they ever.

The phones never stopped ringing from that point forward. My speech became a rallying cry for sick children and CMN told us that the number of donations, and the high dollar amounts of the donations, were far exceeding the norms for those hours of the day. At 11 that morning, the phone company called to apologize and donated $10,000 to Children's Miracle Network. When it was all said and done, we raised well over $300,000 for the Beaumont Children's Hospital. The management of Alice 106.7 and AM/FM was fully supportive of my actions. The incident at the Alice Cares for Kids Radiothon was a watershed moment. I now knew the rest of my radio career and the cause of helping sick children would be intertwined .

When I moved to Raleigh in 2003, my new company Curtis Media Group had started a fledgling radiothon for the Children's Hospital at the University of North Carolina at Chapel Hill. Children's Miracle Network already had a long, established relationship with a hospital in the area and it was a big one – the children's hospital at Duke University was legendary for their care and ground breaking research. They were partners with the heritage adult contemporary station in town, WRAL. But it turned out there was a hospital just a few miles down the road ("Tobacco Road", as sportscasters like to call it come college basketball season, which is 15-501) that also offered great care but was not on the radar. The UNC Children's Hospital is a public operation, meaning no family is denied care regardless of their ability to pay. This hospital was regularly taking in the most severe cases, from trauma occurring in things like car accidents to rare, often incurable illnesses. Their care was so far reaching that they were serving patients from all 100 counties in North Carolina and many parents were driving for hours upon hours to Chapel Hill to receive this care. Yet if you asked a resident of the Triangle what comes to mind when they think of children's hospitals, almost all would talk to you about Duke.

Incredibly, back in 2003 UNC Children's Hospital didn't even have a fundraising arm of the organization nor were they linked to a national charity like CMN to provide guidance. The first radiothon was an effort born of hope and desire, and all the Curtis Media radio stations in North Carolina gathered in the lobby of the hospital to raise money on one day – November 20th. That first radiothon raised over $150,000 with no additional funding and no corporate sponsors. Today, thanks to a decade of experience and amounts raised soaring into the millions, the hospital is thriving with a fully staffed fundraising organization that raises funds through events all year long. During Children's Miracle Network training, you are taught that every radiothon needs a hero. We know that although the air talent can effectively tell stories and share reasons why their listeners should donate money to such a worthwhile cause, it is the children themselves that can transform one of these fundraising events. One thing I've learned from all these radiothons is that sickness forces children to grow up faster than they should and they often overtake their parents in their capacity to handle adversity.

I've met children 7 and 8 years old that are on their second or third round of chemotherapy talking like old souls about their lives, their family, their friends, and their faith.

The hero of my first radiothon at the North Carolina Children's Hospital was Rebecca Simpson. Like my friend Noah, Rebecca was 14 when she was diagnosed with leukemia. The past year had been difficult for her, but the week before Radiothon was a very good one – she learned her cancer had gone into remission. One of the tricks I'd learned from CMN was making vignettes to play throughout the day. We would interview the child and/or the parents, and then find an appropriate song to weave the interview clips through. These could be especially powerful when produced correctly – the words of a child matched with the powerful words of a song could light up phone lines like a Christmas tree. Because Rebecca had received such good news, I elected to use "Beautiful Day" by U2.

Rebecca was the type of person that inspired everyone around her. She was a natural on the radio – she would grab the microphone and take control for hours at a time. She even understood how to tap into the many emotions that triggered a person's propensity to reach into their pocketbook. Sometimes, when the phones weren't ringing, she would scold them. "I don't understand", she would say. "I have cancer and I'm here volunteering – you're healthy and all you have to do is pick up the phone!" Other times she would make deals with the callers. "If someone donates $100 right now, I will do laundry for an entire week." She would take song requests, dedications, send shout outs to her friends, and it was a guarantee that the hours Rebecca joined us on 96rock were the hours during which we raised the most money.

The next couple of years were rollercoasters for Rebecca. Sometimes we'd see her with hair, sometimes we wouldn't.

Sometimes we would see her overweight and puffy from the steroid medications and other times gaunt, thin, and weak. She would beat the cancer, hope would return, and then like a cruel trick it would return stronger than ever. She underwent 12 rounds of chemotherapy, received countless blood transfusions, contracted fungal pneumonia which resulted in two lung surgeries within months of each other, received a bone marrow transplant and fought off graft-versus-host disease. Finally, on February 23, 2007, on the day she graduated high school, Rebecca passed away at home holding her sister's hand.

I went to Rebecca Simpson's funeral, an overwhelming standing room only service that Rebecca herself had planned. I've often thought about faith as it relates to the Simpson family. Rebecca attended North Raleigh Christian Academy and her parents, Jeff and Emmaline, instilled a very strong sense of faith and belief in God within their daughter. Despite losing his daughter years ago, Jeff volunteered all day long at the radiothons with a smile on his face. He is always able to find the positives in life. Jeff will always tell me how thankful he was that Rebecca received her care at that hospital. How amazing the doctors and nurses were. What a special place it is. A lesser person would surely have focused on the fact that their daughter died and the hospital wasn't able to fix her. A lesser person would surely not have been able to maintain a high level of faith in the face of tragedy the way Jeff did. Some say – and I think Jeff and Emmaline would say- that God had a plan for Rebecca. That maybe, just maybe, another angel was needed in heaven. I would like to believe that, but I have a hard time believing that God would want to take a person that was such a positive influence on Earth away from us. Although I have faith in a higher power myself, I can understand where atheists are coming from. On the surface, it's easy to ask, "If there was a God, why is Rebecca dead?" For that matter, if there was a God, would a maniac have walked into an elementary school classroom and killed 20 children? Perhaps God simply gives us free will and He surely cannot stop evil from happening or good people from dying. I just wish it didn't happen to people like Rebecca Simpson.

CHAPTER 39

ST. SHINEDOWN

In March 2004, one of the anchors of the local NBC affiliate, Sharon Delaney, got our station involved with a relatively new charity called St. Baldrick's after losing her infant daughter to cancer. Started on St. Patrick's Day in a bar in New York City, the concept was to raise money for childhood cancer research by shaving one's head (in solidarity for the children who often lose their hair during treatments).

I learned that while many childhood cancer and adult cancers share names, they should not be treated the same. According to the St. Baldrick's Foundation, if every child received childhood cancer treatment instead of adult treatment, 30% more would survive. On their website, St. Baldrick's designates that the funds they raise are not only focused on finding cures, but also used to prevent the lifelong damage that results from surgeries, radiation, and chemotherapies while their bodies and brains are still developing.

Our first year was a small affair, held in the middle bar of the Hibernian Pub in downtown Raleigh. I'm up for about anything and sick kids was one of my hot buttons, so shaving my head (though I had not yet ever done it) was no big deal. That first year, though, one particular scenario moved me.

Dr. Stuart Gold is a children's cancer physician at the North Carolina Children's Hospital and he was sporting very long locks on that day. Rather than a stylist cutting the hair, one person at a time from the crowd was walking up and taking a swipe with the electric razor at Dr. Gold's hair. It became apparent that each of these folks were, at one time, patients of Dr. Gold's in their youth. Now, here they were as adults, attending this event (many with children of their own), thanking Dr. Gold. He saved their lives. Playing music on the radio for a living is fun – but these moments are what make working in radio worth living for. 2017 will mark the 13th straight year I'll be shaving my head to raise funds for St. Baldrick's.

Although this chapter is about the warm feelings of St. Baldrick's, I'd be remiss if I didn't include the Shinedown incident – because it is truly one of the most bizarre moments of my career. In 2009, St. Baldrick's Day at the Hibernian happened to coincide with a concert that night at the Lincoln Theatre by one of the hottest rock bands of the day, Shinedown. Since the St. Baldrick's event was during the day and the concert was at night, I asked the Atlantic Records rep if the band might be able to swing by the Hibernian for an hour. We could sell autographs with all proceeds to St. Baldrick's, I figured, and it would go a lot farther than your typical backstage meet and greet.

The rep arrived with the band in a van, and they made their way to a table under a tent in the street where the shaving was taking place. For the first 45 minutes of their appearance, everything went perfectly according to plan. The rep remarked at how well things were going. Then, one of the members of the band, the dreadlocked drummer Barry Kerch, was so moved by the cause that he decided to cut one of his locks off and make a significant donation to St. Baldrick's. What happened next was unexpected – in part, because I did not plan for security. I didn't anticipate needing security at a charity event, and let's face it – this was Shinedown, not The Beatles.

One patron who clearly had too much to drink inconceivably started giving Barry a hard time about cutting only one lock of his hair instead of all of it, as most St. Baldrick's participants do. This started escalating to the point where I looked at the rep, she looked back at me with a knowing glance, and we grabbed the guys from Shinedown and started walking them out of the tent and towards their van. This guy follows us until we get steps out of the tent and, while he's still yelling, takes a swing at one of the band members. This results in Brent, the lead singer, whisking around and throwing a punch back at drunk guy. Meanwhile, a lovely charity event for kids with cancer is taking place, in full view of us, steps away. One woman was screaming at the top of her lungs, "This is a charity event for children!!! What's the matter with you?? Get out of here!!! Get out of here!!!!" We tried to get them out of there, except that drunk guy wouldn't stop trash talking and more scuffling ensued. "Get out of here! Animals!!!", this woman is yelling and, as the rep finally gets her band back in the van, she is talking to herself. "Oh my god, oh my god, what do I do." She knows she has to call her boss, and she feels like she's going to be reprimanded or fired because she let Shinedown get into a fight on her watch. And what if they're injured? They have a show that night! Meanwhile I'm freaking out because I was the one that asked for the band to come to the Hibernian in the first place. I didn't get security, so really I was the one who let this happen. My station was not going to look good, I was afraid. She said she was going to call her boss, get the band back to the hotel and would call me later.

When she called later, she had spent the afternoon on the phone with her boss (who was very understanding) and the Raleigh Police Department, which took details of the incident. But at that point it seemed everything had settled down so I said, "Do you have time for dinner and drinks before the show?", to which she replied, "I think that's just what I need."

After a terrific dinner at Raleigh's Duck and Dumpling in Moore Square, we walked over to the Lincoln Theatre for the sold out Shinedown show which was already a couple of songs in. I was delighted to see that Barry was wearing a St. Baldrick's t-shirt – so while he was obviously still angry at drunk guy, he was clearly so moved by the event that he wore the shirt at his show. It was an incredible performance to a sold out house which was going perfectly until the encore when guitarist Zach Myers swung his axe around...and accidentally hit lead singer Brent Smith in the face. Give Brent credit – despite blood gushing from his forehead, he finished the song without missing a beat (thank goodness it was the last song). 5 minutes later, my cell phone rang. It was the rep, and she was even more frantic with a side of fatigue and exasperation this time. "Brent cut his forehead open", she said. "What hospital should I take them to?" "Duke Raleigh is the closest", I told her, thinking they would avoid the craziness of Wake Med or Rex at that time of the night and I was right. The next day she said they didn't have to wait long, Brent was stitched up just fine, and it was on to the next city. But I'll bet Shinedown will never forget that charity event they did for that radio station in Raleigh.

CHAPTER 40

YEAH, WE'RE WITH THE BAND

One afternoon I was contacted by Ellington Studios in the tiny town of Angier, NC, located 45 minutes south of Raleigh (at that point I had no earthly idea where Angier was). Rick Ellington, the owner of the studio, wanted to know – did any of our DJs play any instruments?

Remarkably, though the music industry was our chosen profession, not one of the full-time air staff played an instrument. Perhaps it wasn't altogether surprising, since radio DJs live somewhat vicariously through bands. We may not play in them, but we get to introduce them, hang with them backstage, see them perform for free. That's not such a bad deal. But as huge music fans, it's not a reach to say that playing in a band was a lifelong fantasy for many of us. When I brought up the idea of taking lessons at Ellington to the team, it was amazing how easily everything fell into place. As a karaoke junkie, I was the natural choice for lead vocalist (not that I was going to give anyone else a chance anyway). Our morning hosts, Salt and Demetri, would learn lead and rhythm guitar. Midday jock Alli Morgan would learn the bass. The most obvious match of DJ to instrument was that of night jock Adam-12, who would regularly break out in air drumming sessions that resembled something between a convulsion and a seizure. With everyone on board, we began weekly lessons at Ellington with our primary teacher, the excellent Daniel Anderson.

Over the course of the next six months, our band learned the basics of our instruments (I was taking guitar lessons in addition to practicing vocals). We slowly formulated a setlist, focusing on four songs. "Smoke on the Water" by Deep Purple; "Mary Jane's Last Dance" by Tom Petty; "Can't You See" by Marshall Tucker Band, and "Sweet Home Alabama" by Lynyrd Skynyrd. That upcoming January, Raleigh was getting set to host its first NHL All-Star game and the city was planning a giant downtown street celebration called "All-Star Wide Open". Since local bands were playing and I had a working relationship with the guy who books the bands, I did something a little nuts – I asked if we could play the festival. "Really?", Taylor Traversari (the band booker) exclaimed. "We would LOVE to have you play the festival! That would be awesome! We'll give you an hour slot!" An hour? "Well....our set list won't be that long – how about fifteen minutes?", I asked. He laughed. "No problem. We'll give you a half hour and if you finish early, no big deal." Oh, we'd finish early. And one other thing – I had to tell my bandmates that I just committed us to the play the biggest street festival of the year and we barely knew four songs.

Fortunately, my band was up for the challenge. Not only was it personally exciting, but it would be a great promotion for the radio station. We would post videos of our lessons at Ellington, so listeners could follow our progress. We'd talk about it on the air, and mobilize listeners to attend the concert. On the night before the show, I started to feel a sore throat coming on. "You've got to be kidding me", I said to my wife. "Now? The night before the show?" "Get some rest", she told me. "You'll feel better in the morning."

Not only did I not feel better in the morning, I couldn't sing. I couldn't talk. I had completely lost my voice. Amidst flashes of panic, I hunted on the internet for sore throat remedies and I found something with whiskey, honey, and vinegar that I hoped would calm my throat and my nerves. When we arrived downtown for the show, I had a scarf wrapped around my neck and I could still barely talk. I swooped into the corner coffee shop and asked for hot tea with honey. I used hand signals when people approached to talk to me, as I didn't want to risk saying a thing. The symptoms weren't aided by the fact that it was a 38 degree winter day.

When the band before us finished, the team from Ellington flew into action, and it was awesome. We had our own roadies! They set up all our equipment, tuned our guitars and had everything ready for us when we were to walk on the stage. Only problem was, I honestly didn't know if I'd be able to sing. I did vocal exercises at the side of the stage, but until we broke into that first song it was a complete wild card. Plus, the opening song, "Sweet Home Alabama", required me to hit the higher part of my register so I could crack right out of the gate. Looking out amongst the crowd, we noticed the audience had swelled from about 30 people for the previous band to nearly 200 for us. I was a nervous wreck. Finally, it was time to go on. "Sweet Home Alabama" was the one song I played guitar on while I sang (not easy to do) – but it was time, and Salt played the shaky opening notes and we were off and running. "Big wheels keep on turnin...." I hit em! Once I got the first lyrics out of the way, I was able to relax a bit and I stopped thinking about my throat. I could tell the notes were a little shaky, but they would suffice. I had very little interaction with the crowd, mostly because I didn't want to waste my voice at all – and the last song, "Smoke on the Water", was the hardest one to sing. But I plowed through it, we got a nice response, and the video remains on Youtube to this day for all to see. Search "96rock Radiowave". Don't miss my harmonica playing on "Mary Jane's Last Dance"!

Obviously I wish the sore throat incident could have been avoided, but Radiowave (the listeners named the band in a contest) was one of my favorite radio experiences.

Unfortunately, following the big gig, interest in making the 45 minute drive each way started to wane and not long after the station changed direction and we had to let Salt, Demetri and Adam go. Perhaps a Radiowave reunion will be in the cards sometime down the road. Every band has to reunite at some point, right?

CHAPTER 41

NEVER HOST A BATTLE OF THE BANDS

If there was anything in the world that has no upside for the organizer, it is a battle of the bands. The New York Yankees would have more upside playing my eleven year old's baseball team during the regular season than I would in organizing and hosting a battle of the bands competition. There would be more upside in driving a nail through my knuckles than organizing and hosting a battle of the bands competition. You know those scenes on "The Voice" where a singer belts out their tune for 90 seconds and no chairs turn around? Then the judges offer thoughtful constructive criticism and the singer really, really takes it to heart and says, "Thank you so much for the advice. I'm going to keep working hard and will never give up"? Yeah, that doesn't happen in real life. The scenes on "American Idol" where the singer freaks out and blames the judges? Right. That's what happens.

Now to be fair, all the talent on "The Voice" is relatively high level so the musicians know how to take criticism. It is the local musicians with average talent at best that really, truly in their heart of hearts believe they are so close to being signed to a major record label if they are just given that one shot – it is these musicians that make up the vast majority of battle of the bands contests. On one level, I admire their gumption. In a business as cutthroat and ruthless as the music industry, you have to have a certain amount of swagger and confidence that is greater than your ability. The A&R Rep for Sire Records says that when he listened to Madonna's demo tape for the first time, he thought she was "good, but not great". But, he continued, "I knew a superstar was sitting across from me".

But what happens when your talent is so obviously marginal?

During one year that 96rock hosted a battle of the bands competition, the mother of one of the band's singers came over to the judges table and started cursing at us. "You bastards wouldn't know talent if it bit you in the ass! What are your qualifications anyway? Who the fuck are you? Huh? *He's* in a band. A BAND. What are you doing with *your* life, judging so high and mighty over here?" Amazingly, even though her son was clearly in earshot of mommie dearest, he made no attempt to mollify her tirade. A stupid decision, because we actually liked his band very much. As "American Idol" and "The Voice" have shown, winning isn't everything. It's the contacts you make and the exposure you get from the competition that matters. Chris Daughtry, Clay Aiken, and Carrie Underwood were all runner-ups on "American Idol" and have had far superior careers to Lee Dewyze or Taylor Hicks. I know for a fact I would have used this band for station events and recommended them when my contacts at local clubs call in search of local bands to open for national acts. But now, after soap opera central, all bridges are burned and I will in fact go out of my way to tell anyone who will listen to avoid booking the band- lest mommy shows up!

That same year, a group of fans accosted me next to the elevator in a dark parking garage across the street from the venue after their favorite band came in second. These people were spitting in my face, yelling about how this band was the greatest the Triangle has ever seen. And it was a...wait for it....COVER BAND. You know what, assholes? Take that passion you have following a band that makes a living singing 3 Doors Down songs every night and put it towards something that matters. Who knows, maybe we could eradicate hunger or bring about world peace.

Then there was the time I made a terrible error in

judgment when booking one of the bands. It was the third year of the contest, and it was getting harder to find good local bands. So I contacted my friend Amy Cox at Deep South Entertainment and asked for suggestions on some local bands to call and she gave me the number of a guy who is the singer in a local hard rock band. I reached the guy – seemed nice enough – and we booked him for one of the rounds.

I remember when he came up to me at the club, telling me about how their band was so close to getting signed to Roadrunner Records (right). He was obnoxious, arrogant, and certainly overconfident, but he also had an endearing quality to him. He seemed genuinely appreciative of the opportunity the station had given him. And that was all well and good until his band didn't win and he started calling me to find out why he didn't win and could we book his band for station events and – oh- could we play his band's music on the air. None of that was the problem. That kind of behavior happens all the time. The problem was that he had called me....on my cell phone. How did he get...oh no. I did this. It's my fault. I called him that night when I was looking for a band from my cell phone! How could I have been so careless!

Over the ensuing months, he would call every few weeks – like the time he called me at midnight to invite me to one of their shows that was coming up down the road. Or the time he called to tell me he was sending me an mp3 of their new demo. I would politely try to tell him things like, "You know, I have a family, please don't call me at midnight." Or, "Can you please e-mail me instead of calling my cell phone?" But it didn't matter. It never mattered because he kept calling.

Then, one night, his band was booked on a show we were promoting. They were one of the opening bands for Sebastian Bach, former lead vocalist for Skid Row. I was standing at the side of the stage when Sebastian walked off after his performance. It was an emotional moment, because Sebastian had recently lost his home in New Jersey to a storm and was going to move to Los Angeles. We had listeners sign a giant "Best Wishes" greeting card and one listener had donated a beautiful engraved crystal plaque which we presented to him on stage that night. As I'm telling Sebastian how the idea came about and he's thanking me up and down for the thought, this guy walks right in the middle of our conversation and says to Sebastian Bach, "Hey Sebastian, we were your opening band tonight." Despite the fact that he was interrupted, he offers a gracious, "Oh cool, thanks." This guy wasn't done. "How come you didn't mention us on stage?" Sebastian gets a look of indignance and my jaw is on the floor. I literally had to bend over and pick my jaw up off the sticky floor. "What?", he said. "We opened for you and it's common courtesy to thank the opening band. How come you didn't do that?" I've never seen anything like this. I've seen local bands that thought they were the shit, but to completely torpedo any sense of decorum with a platinum selling recording artist...with a temper...."Who the fuck are you?" "We're...", he tries to interject. Sebastian continues, voice rising with every syllable. "I don't care who the fuck you are! You are nobody. NOBODY. You opened for me. This is my show. Get the fuck off my stage. Asshole." I was sure he was going to take a swing at local band douche, but now security was escorting him off the stage. I just wanted to hug Sebastian Bach because he said everything I think about when I rue doing a battle of the bands.

Remember the singer of the band that has my cell phone number? Well, that was his drummer that made a fool of himself in front of Sebastian Bach. And me, being too nice a guy, decided to call the singer to tell him what happened in case he didn't know (which he didn't, he had already left.) I thought to myself, if I was in a band, and I found out that one of my members was representing my product that way in front of influential decision makers and a platinum selling recording artist, I would be really pissed. When I told him, do you know what he said to me? He called me a liar. Questioned my motives in accusing this guy. Thought maybe I had it out for his band. Just do yourself a favor. Never host a battle of the bands. Like ever.

CHAPTER 42

ROGER WATERS APOLOGIZES TO ME

I was not the biggest Pink Floyd fan growing up. In fact, I didn't start listening to Floyd until college and didn't develop a significant appreciation for their music until working at 96rock and playing it regularly. When the remastered version of "The Wall" reached my mailbox, I was hooked and listened to it over and over again. I connected with that album in a way I have not with any other Pink Floyd recording much less any others. When my grandfather passed, I listened to Side 2 of "The Wall" on the drive to the hospital. Unfortunately, I never got to see the band live as their final tour was in 1994, before I would have been interested in buying tickets. Plus, Roger Waters was not in the lineup in that incarnation of the band. When Waters announced he would be presenting a production of 'The Wall" to tour around the world, I felt this was a show I must see somehow, some way.

My mother was also interested in seeing the concert, but there was no stop close to Raleigh. The nearest dates on the first leg of the tour were Atlanta (6 hours away), and Washington DC (a 4 ½ hour drive). The idea was for my mother to fly to the east coast where I would meet her for one of the shows. One day my mom called and threw a curveball to the plan. "With my job, I'm just not going to be able to make it to the east coast", she said. "Why don't you come out to the show in Oakland." The tour had added a Friday night show in the Bay Area, so I could fly out and see my mom and go to the show. Problem with that scenario was that there was no way I could afford airfare and a ticket to the concert. "If I buy my airline ticket, will you get the concert tickets?", I inquired. "Yes", she responded. Well, that was easy. "They are expensive.", I mentioned. They were especially expensive even for a production of this magnitude. But I knew that my mother was not going to buy nosebleed seats. If she's going to a Roger Waters show, she's going all the way. "With service fees, it's $250 a ticket", I said matter-of-factly. Ouch. Silence. "Where would the seats be?", she wanted to know. "Hold on", I said, and started clicking away on the Ticketmaster site to see what $250 would get you on this day. "They are really good seats. First section back from the stage, about ten rows up. Perfect." "Do it", she announced and gave me her credit card number to get the transaction done. That night I booked my flight and the trip was planned for the weekend of my 38th birthday.

The tickets were print-at-home, so I had the regular size paper folded in my pocket with the barcodes printed on them. Mom and I walked to the proper gate where the ticket taker scanned my ticket. "Hmmm.", she said. "Umm, sorry for the inconvenience, but you're going to have to go to the box office please and show them your ticket there." Uh-oh. Had I been scammed by a counterfeit site? I'd hear stories about this. It looks exactly like the Ticketmaster site but in fact it's some third party that the browser has routed to. After all this, the money for the tickets, my airfare, the travel, it's going to come down to this.

We walked to the box office, where I told the gentleman how the ticket taker wouldn't accept our tickets and we had to come see him. He looked good and hard at our tickets for a very long 30 seconds. "Hold on please", he said as he disappeared into a back room. Oh god, we're going to get arrested now! My mother is just staring at me, wondering how I could have possibly screwed up such a simple task as buying concert tickets. A different box office man came back. "Roger wants to send his deepest apologies", this man explained. "Upon review of tonight's layout, your original seats were too close to the pyrotechnics Roger will use in the show tonight. So he's made arrangements for you to have these seats instead. He hopes you have a wonderful time." "Ok, thank you", I replied, just relieved that I wasn't going to be dragged off to the klink. I signed a piece of paper, looked down at the stubs in my hand, and noticed that under "Section", was the word "Floor". Under row was the letter "B". I looked down at the tickets, then looked up at my mother. Down at the tickets again, then up at my mother. "I think these are good seats", I told her.

In we went, to the floor, to the center section, to the center of the second row, right in front of the stage. It was the greatest rock show I have seen to this day. A year and a half later the tour would finally make a stop in Raleigh, which I took my wife to see. It was as awesome as the first time if not better – but it wasn't in the second row.

CHAPTER 43

ROBIN WILLIAMS WAS MY CHEERLEADER

Over the years, 96rock cultivated a remarkable relationship with the people at the Durham Performing Arts Center, one of the top 5 theatres for attendance in the world. A high level of mutual trust has resulted in a string of fun, creative promotions that most venues or promoters would not ever attempt or approve and a level of unparalleled success for the theater that has made it one of the most successful and admired.

It was this level of trust that, when David Steinberg's people sent a letter to DPAC asking for a popular local radio personality to introduce Robin Williams and David Steinberg at their upcoming show, Emily at DPAC asked if I was interested. You know who Robin Williams is of course, and David Steinberg is keenly aware that, if you are under the age of 50, you probably don't know who he is. Some research will reveal his most startling career statistic – besides Bob Hope, no guest appeared on "The Tonight Show with Johnny Carson" more than David Steinberg. On top of that, he was the youngest guest host in the history of the show (he would go on to guest host 12 times). In his heyday as a stand-up comedian in the 60's and 70's, David Steinberg was groundbreaking. He was responsible for getting The Smothers Brothers variety TV show removed from the schedule thanks to some religious humor the network thought was far too edgy for the time. In the 80's Steinberg moved behind the camera, and was responsible for writing and directing a great many episodes of some of the best sitcoms of the last few decades. These shows have included 'Seinfeld", "Mad About You", "Friends", and "Curb Your Enthusiasm".

Without hesitation, I accepted the invitation to introduce the show. A request for a radio personality to intro a show is very unusual. We view concert intros as outstanding promotional opportunities. We get to talk to a captured audience, get them fired up for the show, and get credit for the station's brand. We always have to ask for approval for a stage intro, and it is up to the artist management whether or not it happens – which, more times than not, it does not.

Long-time friends Robin Williams and David Steinberg were on a sit-down comedy tour. Rather than a traditional stand-up comedy show, this was an interview format that would feature Robin Williams riffing on his entire career from "Mork and Mindy" to stand-up to the many great films to his credit. I was told to arrive at the venue by 7:30pm and meet Marketing Director Emily, which I did. Showtime on the ticket was 8pm. I asked her what the plan was for the evening. "I'm not really sure", she told me. "I think they have a script." A script was also extremely unusual. There is the rare instance where you're given a few copy points to mention in a stage intro, but generally speaking the content is up to you. The exception is charity events, when you are almost always handed a script filled with sponsor names you have to mention over and over again. Radio talent, not having to rely on teleprompters for their delivery, tend to be very good at ad-libbing and coming up with material off the cuff. "No problem", I said regarding the script, and we made our way to the DPAC backstage area.

The striking feature of the backstage area of the Durham Performing Arts Center is the wall, which is signed by most of the performers that have played the venue. While Emily and I were waiting for further instructions and the script, I made note of Whoopi Goldberg's signature on the wall. I knew Whoopi was there the night before and, knowing that Robin Williams and Whoopi Goldberg were longtime friends, wondered if she would be a special guest on this evening. Emily explained that nearly half of the audience didn't show up for Whoopi's show the previous night due to perilous weather - and that Whoopi's bus showed up just a couple hours before the show was to begin (she does not like to fly). She did not stay in town, because she had to return to New York City for a show she was part of on Saturday night. It was at exactly this part of the story when we hear a familiar (and loud) voice emanating from the hallway around the corner. "Whoopi was here last night?", says the voice. "Fuck off!" With that, a mustached Robin Williams pops out of his dressing room and appears before us. "Wow", Robin muses. "I had no idea she was here." As with most conversations with Robin Williams, I imagine, the topic drifts to something else entirely - the sprinklers on the ceilings. Emily reveals a moment when the sprinklers all went off in the building, nearly causing loads of irreparable damage. "Oh, that happened when we were filming Bicentennial Man", Robin tells us. "We were shooting a scene in San Francisco, when we triggered the sprinkler system and we had to pay for all kinds of damage. They weren't happy with us and we weren't allowed to shoot there anymore." I was particularly curious now, since I grew up in San Francisco. "What building was it?", I asked. With a smirk, Robin replied, "City Hall".

Now a much younger looking than his age David Steinberg pops out of his dressing room, looks my way and inquires, "Are you the radio guy?" I affirmed that I was. "Great", he says, handing me a single sheet of paper. "Here is a script. Look it over for a few minutes, then we'll discuss it." It was essentially a brief biography of Steinberg, to alert the audience to the accolades he's achieved and shows he's worked on over the years. After a few minutes of review, Steinberg said, "Follow me", and escorted me into his dressing room.

Steinberg asked me a little bit about my radio station, then gave me permission to ad-lib a bit from the script. "Feel free to put some of this in your own words", he instructed. "At the end, you'll say 'And here's the guy he'll be talking to tonight', and a short movie about Robin's career will begin on the screen above you." "Perfect", I said. Since we had a few more minutes, I asked him about "Curb Your Enthusiasm", complimenting him on what I think is one of the greatest comedies of all time. He told me he was fairly certain Larry David was going to sign on for another season and debunked one of the greatest myths about the show. "It's not improv at all", he told me. "That show is so tightly scripted but the actors are so good, they make it seem like it's completely improvised, like everyone thinks it is. But it's not." It was just a couple minutes til 8 and was time for me to make my way to the stage, where I was handed a wireless mic. A large man that was part of the crew asked, "Are you nervous"? "Yeah, a little", I told him. "Because I'm such a fan". I'd done so many of these stage announcements and it's not like I haven't been a fan of many of the artists I've introduced, but this was one of the biggest comedians of all time and it had an intimate feel that none of the others did (I'd just hung out with them backstage). The board operator gave me the green light and spoke in his headset to someone else behind the curtain. "DJ coming out".

The introduction went perfectly. I briefly introduced myself, and then found a way to really play up David Steinberg's resume. I said, "You may not have known the name David Steinberg before you saw it on your ticket, but I'll bet you know some of the shows he's worked on. Anyone ever hear of 'Seinfeld'?", and of course an impressed batch of oohs and ahhs rose up from the audience as well as a round of applause. "How about Friends?", I continued. I continued with this approach, rolling through his other shows including "Mad About You" and "Curb Your Enthusiasm". The crowd was very impressed when I told them only Bob Hope had appeared more on "The Tonight Show with Johnny Carson". Finally it was time for my finale and I said, "And tonight, David Steinberg will be talking to this guy", and I pointed up to the movie screen with one last line that timed perfectly with the start of the film. "Enjoy the show!"

I turned to walk back to stage right, where I immediately saw David Steinberg grinning on the right and another man jumping up and down with his arms stretched widely to the sky on the left. It was Robin Williams. "You were great, chief", he told me. "Very nicely done", Steinberg added. The show was just wonderful. Different than a stand-up routine but better in many ways because it was so intimate and provided remarkable insight into both men's careers and personal lives, I enjoyed it immensely. After the show we were invited to Robin's meet and greet in which he again told me what a good job I had done. Without any prompting, he looked down to sign a photo for me and wrote, "To Jay. You Did Great. Robin Williams". This was one of the greatest nights of my life.

When Robin committed suicide on August 11th, 2014, one day after my 17th wedding anniversary, I was sitting at the pool with my bride. We learned when a push alert beeped on our phones at the same time.

CHAPTER 44

JOEY, EVER BEEN IN A...TURKISH PRISON?

There's always been no doubt that the best perks of my job are the music related ones. Going to concerts, meeting many of my idols backstage, broadcasting from the Grammys...all of these things have made radio an incredible career choice. Sometimes the best perks are the ones you least expect, as was the case when one of our salespeople at Radio 96.1 asked me if I'd be interested in flying a plane.

I would have spit out what my brain was thinking, which was, "YES, YES, YES!!!" Like so many children, I dreamt one day of being a pilot. While it was never a serious career path consideration, I did bring it up to my wife as a hobby option but was usually discouraged when the cost of such a hobby was taken into account. The initial thought I had when the sales rep brought it up to me was what my wife would think from a safety standpoint. I'd thought about skydiving before – "Nope", she would say. Parasailing? "Forget it", was the response. Hangliding? "Out of the question". As the years went on, I adopted her position too. Now that we had children, a tragedy while participating in a hobby like that would be a stupid way to leave this world. I did not know how she'd react to the possibility of flight when I brought it up in November 2012.

As local celebrities, radio personalities are offered the chance to do endorsements. Endorsements are awesome because you get paid to endorse the product, and occasionally you get complimentary use of the product. This comes in quite handily when, for example, you endorse Time Warner

Cable. I've endorsed a wide range of products, from a computer training center to restaurants to a jewelry store to a local brewery. I did not ever expect to be offered the chance to endorse a flight school. If you're going to do that, you really should experience it for yourself..don't you think?

When my wife gave the green light, I made an appointment for what's called the "Discovery Flight" at Blue Line Aviation. I don't know about you, but when I pictured what a first flight lesson would entail, it wasn't much more than the instructor taking off, showing me some of the basics, and then perhaps letting me take the wheel for a few minutes. It was quite the surprise, then, when I was taxiing the Cessna 172 to the runway myself – learning that you steer the plane on the ground with your feet on the pedals which takes quite a bit of getting used to. Once we made our way to the runway, I was pulling back on the throttle and when we reached a certain speed (all I could think of, as a 'Back to the Future' nut was 88 miles per hour) I was pulling back on the wheel (the "elevator" in aviation-speak). What an initial rush when you are lifting the plane off the ground! Everything about the experience is exhilarating, including air traffic control giving you instructions in your headset, like telling you to climb from 2500 to 3000 feet. Heck, I would have done it just to get the awesome Facebook profile pic of me wearing the headset in the pilot's seat. In that first lesson, I did climbs and descents and there was just something insanely awesome about my instructor, Captain Mike, telling me, "See downtown Raleigh over there? Head that way."

While only my initial flight was complimentary, my mother bought me a gift certificate for my birthday and I was able to book my second and third lessons. On the second lesson, I learned how to recover from a stall, a fact I purposely neglected to mention in my Blue Line commercial (I don't

173

think recovering from a stall is a strong selling point!). Can you believe on my second lesson I slowed the plane down to stall speed, allowed the nose to dip and then got it up and running again? "That's fun, right?", remarked Captain Mike. Why, no – not so much fun! How about 45 degree turns in that second lesson, with the full feeling of G forces as I was thrusted back in my seat, pulling back on the elevator while in its steep turn? That was fun. I nearly landed the plane on that second lesson. After Captain Mike told me to line the plane up with the runway at RDU, I started the approach but the crosswinds were quite strong and he said, "I think I'll take it this time for safety." Good call, Captain Mike.

It was on my third and most awesome lesson that I did just about everything. I communicated with the tower, and don't think I didn't use "that voice". The low, elongated vocal pattern that every pilot since the dawn of flight has used to communicate with the passengers. "Raleigh tower, this iiiiis Cessna two three two zero echo, permission to...uh...proceed to runway" After taxi, takeoff, and climbing, we flew to another airport for the first time where Captain Mike noted there was no control tower. I suppose it had never occurred to me that most small airports are self-regulated by the pilots coming in and out of it. As I approached the tiny runway in Louisburg, NC, imagine my surprise when another pilot called out on the radio, "Watch for skydivers in one minute". What? My approach into Louisburg was sketchy at best. Taking off is pretty easy because the tower instructs you to take off into the wind. It is the crosswinds during landings that make it so tricky to navigate a smooth approach. So here I was, attempting my first landing, swerving side to side, holding on to the elevator as tight as I could, wanting to get the plane on the ground before skydivers were apparently going to descend on the airport. With the throttle off, I glided in to the right side of the runway. "Nose up", Captain Mike instructed. As I adjusted the trim, brought the nose up, and then set it down, the landing was remarkably smooth. Until I kept pushing the right rudder instead of the brake (they are on the same pedal!) and nearly ran off the right side of the runway while Captain Mike laughed. You have to have quite the sense of humor (and patience) to be a flight instructor, I would imagine.

As I got my bearings on the brakes, Captain Mike told me to bring the plane to the yellow line, stop, and look up. There did my eyes see a scene straight out of "Honeymoon In Vegas" – fifteen or twenty skydivers opening their parachutes and landing at the airport. After watching the show for ten minutes, I took off back towards Raleigh and a few minutes in resumed communication with the tower at RDU. My approach this time was much smoother. I had a better feel for how to adjust the trim as I kept the runway centered, and was able to follow his instructions in opening the flaps and reducing speed as we made our way in. (It is challenging as a new pilot to remember that the pitch controls speed and power controls altitude on the landing, since your brain assumes it is the other way around).

In the first month of the endorsement with Blue Line Aviation, we sold $10,000 in gift certificates as Christmas gifts using commercials in which I described my personal electric flight experience. Sometimes I only think of the radio experience as one dimensional, as in the music industry. Learning to fly proves it is has been more than that.

CHAPTER 45

SOME OF MY FAVORITE (AND NOT SO FAVORITE) SHOWS

AC/DC – DEC. 18, 2008, TIME WARNER CABLE ARENA, CHARLOTTE

The loudest concert I've ever seen. I know this because my ears rang for two weeks straight. Like, didn't stop ringing, to the point that I went to the doctor and he told me it wasn't permanent and that it would eventually go away and it did. I was scared to death that between all the amplified listening in headphones throughout my radio career and too many concerts to count, I had finally scarred my eardrums beyond recognition thanks to the cannons in "For Those About to Rock". Fantastic show.

AEROSMITH & THE CULT – OCTOBER 25, 2001, THE PALACE OF AUBURN HILLS, DETROIT

It felt strange seeing a rock concert so soon after 9/11, but this was a great one. Awkward moment backstage – I knew Steven Tyler and Joe Perry's names, but the other two not so much. I was given a poster for them to sign and when I went up to Brad Whitford I said, "Excuse me? Excuse me...hey...man..can you sign this for me?" He did begrudgingly after giving me the stink eye.

ALICE COOPER – JUNE 22, 2012, RED HAT AMPHITHEATER, RALEIGH

I don't particularly care for Alice Cooper, but I love a good show. When you pay good money for a concert, the people should expect more than a singer just standing there. Even though Alice has been around a long time, he sounded great and put on a terrific show – full of the blood and assorted effects you'd expect.

ALICE IN CHAINS – APRIL 21, 2010, MEMORIAL AUDITORIUM, RALEIGH

This venue has decent acoustics for musicals, but overmodulated rock concerts sound terrible. Not my favorite band, and William Duval is a reasonable stand in for Layne Staley, but didn't do much for me.

ALTER BRIDGE – JULY 12, 2008, MOORE SQUARE, RALEIGH

As part of our Downtown Live series, we brought the members of Creed minus Scott Stapp to town. My co-host Bob the Blade asked guitarist Mark Tremonti if he could ever see Creed getting back together and he vehemently said no. They did, not long after.

BB KING – JANUARY 18, 2002, FOX THEATER, DETROIT

BB King was old for a long time. He told the crowd at the legendary Fox that night that he was gonna sit down and play his guitar Lucille, because he's old and he can do whatever he wants. Shows in his last few years of life saw King barely able to get through a performance – I'm lucky to have seen him while he still was able to give it his all. The King of the Blues passed away in 2015 at age 89.

BILLY JOEL – MARCH 12, 1996, UNIVERSITY OF SCRANTON CULTURAL CENTER, SCRANTON, PA

I've seen Billy many times, in stadiums and arenas, but only once with my friend Alicia in a tiny venue the size of the Scranton Cultural Center. It was a stop on his "Words and Music Tour", and it was special. Billy told stories behind the music, introduced the Philadelphia DJ who first played "Captain Jack" on the FM dial (who was in the audience that night), took requests, let a kid come up and sing with him...those kind of shows are once in a lifetime.

BON JOVI – DECEMBER 21, 1995, COUNT BASIE THEATER, RED BANK, NJ

I've seen Bon Jovi twice – once at the Palace of Auburn Hills in your prototypical 20,000 arena, and once at the Count Basie Theater in Jon Bon Jovi's hometown of Red Bank, New Jersey. Theater capacity: 1,543. Since 1990, the band has played an annual Christmas show for charity at this intimate venue and it was it was a rare ticket indeed. There were lots of things that made this show special – the size of the hall, the fact that he played covers you'd never see him play at an arena or stadium show (including "Tumbling Dice" by the Stones and "Heaven Help Us All" by Stevie Wonder), and of course the after party at a pool hall down the street at which I played a game of 8-ball with Richie Sambora. He won, but I'd say I was the winner that night.

BRUCE SPRINGSTEEN – AUGUST 14, 1992, THE CENTRUM, WORCESTER, MA

"WOOSTER" as the Boss calls Worcester, this was my favorite of all Springsteen shows I've seen – despite it being without the E Street Band. It was my first time seeing him, it was 3 hours and 45 minutes long, it was loaded with songs I love like "Darlington County" and "Darkness on the Edge of Town", and I was there with two of my fraternity brothers and best friends so I'm sure that biased the experience. I would get to see Bruce with the E Street Band in Buffalo for 1999's reunion tour and Raleigh in 2014 when his daughter Jessica, who goes to Duke, danced on stage during "Dancing In The Dark" (a la Courtney Cox in the video).

COLDPLAY – AUGUST 6, 2009, TIME WARNER CABLE MUSIC PAVILION, RALEIGH

I swear everyone we knew was at this show and Coldplay did what Coldplay does. Large bouncing glowing balls and excessive dramatic lighting, oh my! I found it kind of boring.

CREED – SEPTEMBER 5, 2012, DURHAM PERFORMING ARTS CENTER, DURHAM

Funny, when Creed reunited I thought this show at the intimate DPAC would be a no-brainer booking. This was a band that sold out arenas and amphitheaters in the day – but they sold less than 1,500 tickets that night.

DAVE MATTHEWS BAND – MAY 11, 1996, MASSEY HALL, TORONTO

It's challenging to choose which DMB show to highlight since I've seen them more than any other band, over 30 times. In the period between 1995 and 2000, my wife and I went to any Dave Matthews show within a reasonable driving distance. This show in the intimate legendary Toronto venue featured G Love and Special Sauce as the opening band, and G Love sat in with DMB during their set. I'll never forget waiting outside to get in because it was snowing (on May 11th!)

and it was hot as Hades inside. This was one of Dave's epically long shows – about 3 ½ hours.

DAVID BOWIE – AUGUST 6, 2002, DTE ENERGY MUSIC THEATER, DETROIT

It kills me that the first and only time I saw David Bowie was when he opened – opened – for Moby on Moby's Area 2 tour. When you see an artist like Bowie, you want more than a one hour set but what a set it was. In front of a simple glittering sign that said, "Bowie", he opened with "Life on Mars", played "Ashes to Ashes", "Ziggy Stardust", "Heroes", "Fame"....Bowie proved he was as good as ever. I could have never predicted his last concert tour would end just two years later, and certainly wouldn't have thought he'd be gone from this Earth before turning 70.

DEF LEPPARD – AUGUST 27, 2007, WALNUT CREEK AMPHITHEATER, RALEIGH

Def Leppard, Styx, and Foreigner were getting ready to play a summer show when an "isolated" storm roared right through the venue. We were broadcasting from the top of the lawn when the wind started howling and we went running for the steps leading down towards the VIP area, where we could get some shelter. As I was crossing the walkway, a metal table whizzed past my head, only a few feet away from my cabeza. They had to postpone the show that night – this was the postponed date. It was also when I first upset the members of Styx by asking them when they were going to play Mr. Roboto again (they don't play it anymore, thanks to a schism with former vocalist Dennis DeYoung).

DURAN DURAN – AUGUST 21, 2012, DURHAM PERFORMING ARTS CENTER, DURHAM

Sometimes you just benefit from seeing a band on their way down. That's not to say Duran Duran is off the radar, but there's a big difference between seeing them in Wembley Stadium and the 2,700 seat DPAC. This show was fantastic and it turned out we were fortunate to catch it – the band cancelled their 9 remaining tour dates right after the DPAC show after keyboardist Nick Rhodes came down with a suspected viral infection. They played their cover of Grandmaster Flash's "White Lines", which I happen to love.

EMF – NOVEMBER 20, 1991, GOLDSTEIN AUDITORIUM, SYRACUSE, NY

A one-hit wonder if there ever was one, EMF had a monster hit on the charts called "Unbelievable" that used a sample of Andrew Dice Clay's signature "Oh!!!" in the hook. In the first half of my sophomore year, the band played a gig in the acoustically horrific Goldstein Auditorium inside the Schine Student Center on the campus of Syracuse University. My friend Jon Marsh knew some super-secret way to navigate the back annals of the venue to access the dressing room, so he proposed a not-so-bright idea to take that tour prior to the show. The hallway was dark and the turns were like something out of "Spinal Tap", but all of a sudden there we were in EMF's dressing room as they were getting ready for the show – wearing nothing but their skivvies (if that). They screamed at us to get the fuck out of there, which we did in short order, and its only for the lax security that we weren't escorted out of the building immediately.

ELTON JOHN & BILLY JOEL – JULY 17, 1994, FOXBOROUGH STADIUM, FOXBOROUGH, MA

I've seen Elton and Billy three times, Elton by himself three times, and Billy solo four times – but this was the first of many "Face to Face Tours" Elton and Billy would do together. We had seats in 10th row center and Elton and Billy were electric that night – many times artists tour together but never perform together, and it was a delight to see both of them start the show by singing "Your Song", "Honesty", and "Don't Let the Sun Go Down on Me" together. I loved the format of them singing together, then an Elton set, then a Billy set, then both together again, with each singing each other's songs. It was refreshing and really fun.

ELVIS COSTELLO – APRIL 29, 2012, DURHAM PERFORMING ARTS CENTER, DURHAM, NC

I had seen Elvis once before, at DTE Energy Music Theater (a large amphitheater) in Detroit in the early part of the 21st century and I found it pretty darn boring. I remember thinking that Elvis was hardly engaged with the audience and that the venue was much too vast and cavernous for a singer-songwriter like Costello. It was the wrong vibe entirely.

Cut to 2012 as Elvis was playing the final U.S. show of his "Revolving Setlist Tour". Starring Elvis as a carnival barker with a giant spinning wheel that audience members would spin to determine which song he'd play next and an on-stage cage where concert-goers could go-go dance, this was absolutely one of the most enjoyable, spontaneous, and joyous shows I've ever seen. He and his incredibly accomplished band, The Imposters, tore through 36(!) songs over 3 hours and 45 minutes – a Bruce Springsteen-esque marathon that included hits, rarities, and covers. Concerts do not get much better than this.

GOO GOO DOLLS – OCTOBER 8, 1995, CLUB CHAMELEON, SYRACUSE, NY

You would think it absurd now, but over twenty years ago a Goo Goo Dolls show was a sweaty, thrashing, mosh pit laden adventure. It was, in fact, the only mosh pit I've ever partaken in (no crowd surfing or stage diving, but definitely a few battle wounds). The Goos were just becoming a household name thanks to their first hit, "Name" from "A Boy Named Goo". But with hometown Buffalo only a couple hours away, the Goo Goo Dolls tore through that club with beautiful reckless abandon. I hate to say it, but I find seeing them now incredibly boring. They evolved from a hard rock outfit with pop sensibilities (a la The Replacements) to a soccer mom band. Not that there's anything wrong with that, and they sure cashed in. I'm just glad I got the chance to see them when….

GREEN DAY – DECEMBER 7, 2004, THE JOINT AT THE HARD ROCK CAFÉ, LAS VEGAS, NV

Green Day, on my birthday, playing "American Idiot" in its entirety, in a club, the night before I attended the Billboard Music Awards. That didn't suck.

LENNY KRAVITZ – JUNE 19, 1993, PALACIO DE DEPORTES, MADRID, SPAIN

Lenny was one of my favorite artists ever since I heard "Let Love Rule" while I was interning at X100 in San Francisco. I was studying abroad in the Summer of 1993 and a group of us saw a concert poster of Lenny and I knew I had to go. In that part of the world, things happen later (you take a 3 hour lunch and siesta, after all), and the sun doesn't set until after 10pm in the Summer, so Lenny didn't come on until 10:30. This is when I learned Lenny Kravitz is far bigger in Europe than in the United States – he played songs he'd never play in America...and his set was preceded by the opener, Robert Plant. The lead singer of Led Zeppelin opened for Lenny Kravitz.

MADONNA – MAY 20, 1990, OAKLAND COLISEUM, OAKLAND, CA

Madonna played three consecutive nights in the Bay Area and I believe I saw the final one, a perk of my employment at the Top 40 station in San Francisco. This was Madonna at her peak – the "Blond Ambition Tour", and it was awesome. She divided the show into thematic sets, opening with "Express Yourself", "Open Your Heart", "Causing a Commotion" and "Where's the Party". Then was the "religious" set, in which she treated you to songs like "Like a Prayer", "Papa Don't Preach", and "Live to Tell", a Dick Tracy set, an Art Deco set with "Material Girl", "Vogue", "Cherish" and "Into the Groove", and the encore with "Holiday" and "Keep It Together". These days she's trying to stay young by starting concerts at 11pm and playing just a few hits but it is alienating her fan base. I certainly don't need to see her again – no way she could top it and that's ok.

PAUL MCCARTNEY – APRIL 1, 1990, U.C. BERKELEY MEMORIAL STADIUM, BERKELEY, CA

Another perk of my first radio station gig, this was my first time seeing Paul McCartney and for me, nothing tops The Beatles. This show was a big deal for a number of reasons (including it being my first time seeing him). It was Paul's first major tour since he went on the road with Wings in 1979 and the first tour as Paul McCartney. It was the first tour in which he fully embraced a Beatles-laden setlist. Because the stadium is located in a residential neighborhood, a ban on concerts had to be lifted – and in hippy dippy Berkeley, Paul McCartney was probably the only artist that could have gotten away with it (outside of perhaps the Grateful Dead).

PAUL SIMON, DECEMBER 1, 2011, DURHAM PERFORMING ARTS CENTER, DURHAM, NC

I would have loved to had the chance to see Simon & Garfunkel but I was too young the first time and the reunion tours never seemed to come my way. But seeing Paul Simon in a venue like DPAC with less than 3,000 seats and perfect acoustics (from 5th row center) was simply perfection. The album "Graceland" had just turned 25, and the setlist was markedly pronounced from that recording. All the other songs you'd want to hear were there too, and song thirteen had a profound effect on me. Just ten seconds in, I knew I recognized the song but couldn't place it. I knew it was beautiful, I knew I liked it, but what was it from? Then tears involuntarily just started streaming down my face. It was the most bizarre feeling. It wasn't until I checked the setlist later that I realized why this happened. The song was "The Only Living Boy in New York", a deep track from Simon and Garfunkel's "Bridge Over Troubled Water" album. When I was a little boy (and mama loved me like a rock), I listened to that album to put me to sleep every night and I literally had not heard that song since my childhood. Those notes brought me back to a very happy place in my subconscious. The power of music indeed.

PRINCE – APRIL 19, 1997, SAN JOSE STATE EVENT CENTER ARENA, SAN JOSE, CA

This was my first time seeing the Purple One, and it was after this show that I experienced our bizarre meeting, documented elsewhere in this book.   The show was scintillating – if you can get past the fact that Prince likes to stick his hits in medleys and play full versions of songs you probably don't know, you can't help but be flabbergasted by the man's talent. He played every instrument in concert, was probably the world's most underappreciated guitarist, and for the encore he played three Santana songs.   With Carlos Santana.

CHAPTER 46

SPARE CHANGE

"Everything good that has happened in your life happened because something changed".

I love this quote.

It applies to all good things, like having children, and even things I may have thought were bad at the time that turned out to be good, like getting terminated from a job (the next one was better!)

If someone asked me to describe myself, I wouldn't call myself a risk taker. I suppose that's because I'm not a risk taker in the traditionally thought sense, which may be closer to thrill seeker. I don't feel the need to jump out of a plane tomorrow (though I'd like to someday), I don't need to ride the fastest roller coaster, and you'll probably never see me tackle a Black Diamond slope at a ski resort (never say never!).

But...when I left San Francisco for an overnight job that paid $16,000 a year in Syracuse, New York, that was a risk.

When I conquered my fear of public speaking by addressing a movie theater premiere crowd staring at me for the first time, that was a risk.

When I took a job in San Francisco without having met the Program Director in person or ever set foot in the station, that was a risk.

When I departed arguably the greatest city in the world for Buffalo because I wanted to be at the forefront of a new venture, that was a risk.

When I took a job in Detroit with a new format and having

to build the station from scratch, that was a risk.

When I took a huge pay cut to move to Raleigh because I thought the mission of the company and the people was more important, that was a risk.

When I walked into a conference room at Curtis Media Group in March, 2014 and announced I would be leaving radio to lead the marketing effort at an IT training center, that was a risk.

In April, 2015 I started JayBird Voiceovers for those in need of a contemporary, real, compelling presentation for their products. I am and will forever be in love with radio.

As for the next chapter, I'm writing it every day – and I hope you do too.

"It's good to have an end to journey toward; but it is the journey that matters, in the end."

-Ernest Hemingway

Jay Nachlis was born in Wilkes-Barre, PA where his family owned a furniture store with an incredibly catchy jingle until 1999. He moved to San Francisco at age 5, and really grew up in the City, not like those people that say they're from San Francisco but actually live in Petaluma.

His radio career started with a high school internship, took him to Syracuse University to major in Television, Radio, and Film Management and minor in Spanish, then all over the country. His journey took him from Syracuse, back to San Francisco, across the country to Buffalo, up to Detroit, and finally down to Raleigh, North Carolina where he resides with his wife, two children, two shelties, and a guinea pig named "Squishy".

Nachlis was one of the youngest Program Directors in the United States, and has left an influential mark on the industry. Young talent under his tutelage went on to successful careers in large markets as Program Directors, consultants, marketers, and morning show hosts. He was featured on the cover of Network 40 magazine ("Nice Guys Finish First"), nominated for a Billboard Award, interviewed for BBC World News, and has been a two time guest faculty member at the Kellar Radio Talent Institute at Appalachian State University.

CONTACT THE AUTHOR

For interview requests, reproduction permissions, and other inquiries, please send a detailed e-mail with your contact information to jaybird@jaybirdvoiceovers.com.

To inquire regarding voiceover services, please visit jaybirdvoiceovers.com.

JayBird Voiceovers on Facebook: @jaybirdvoiceovers

Jay Nachlis on Twitter: @talkupthepost

JayBird Voiceovers on Instagram: jaybirdvoiceovers

Printed in Great Britain
by Amazon